"All the coast passed this day is very bold; there is a great swell and the land is very high. There are mountains which seem to reach the heavens, and the sea beats on them; sailing along close to land, it appears as though they would fall on the ships."

Cabrillo

From Cabrillo's first visit in the 1600's, to Henry Miller today, there was always the feeling that the coast was only there temporarily— soon to be reclaimed by the insistent sea. But here was life, while it lasted. The Spanish who built the Old Pacific Capitol were noted for their pride, manners and beautiful voices. They ushered in an era of turbulence and romance, where silver flowed like water and animal hides were used so much in trade that they were known as "California banknotes." On Sunday afternoons bulls fought grizzly bears in outdoor rings, and in the evenings guitars sang out at fandangos throughout the towns.

From the beginning the awesome and magnificent coast beckoned to writers, and they came. Here is a collection of some of their finest works —and a timeless view of Monterey and her citizens.

TALES OF MONTEREY

TALES OF MONTEREY

Davis and Judy Dutton, Eds.

BALLANTINE BOOKS • NEW YORK

For permission to reprint certain selections included in this volume we thank the following:

"Carmel Al Fresco," from *Scenes and Portraits: Memories of Childhood & Youth* by Van Wyck Brooks. Published by E. P. Dutton & Co., Inc. and used with their permission.

"Jeffers," from "Robinson Jeffers: Give Your Heart to the Hawks," in *California Classics* by Lawrence Clark Powell. Copyright © 1971 by Lawrence Clark Powell.

"Boats in a Fog," from *The Selected Poetry of Robinson Jeffers*, copyright 1920 by Robinson Jeffers, copyright renewed 1956. Reprinted by permission of Random House, Inc.

"Hands," from *Dear Judas and Other Poems* by Robinson Jeffers, copyright 1928 by Robinson Jeffers, copyright renewed 1957. Reprinted by permission of Random House, Inc.

"From *Cannery Row*," by John Steinbeck. Copyright 1945 by John Steinbeck, © 1973 by Elain Steinbeck, John Steinbeck IV, and Thomas Steinbeck. Reprinted by permission of The Viking Press, Inc.

"Big Sur," from *Big Sur and the Oranges of Hieronymous Bosch* by Henry Miller. Copyright © by New Directions Publishing Corporation.

SBN 345-24075-8-150

First Printing: June 1974

Printed in the United States of America

Cover photo by Ray Atkeson

A Comstock Edition

BALLANTINE BOOKS
A Division of Random House, Inc.
New York, N.Y. 10022
Simultaneously published by
Ballantine Books, Ltd., Toronto, Canada

CONTENTS

INTRODUCTION

"It is all that can be desired . . . the land has a genial climate, its waters are good." The words are those of the explorer Sebastian Vizcaíno telling the King of Spain what he found at the place he named Monterey in the year 1602.

Alter the language a little, and that message could have been penned on the back of a postcard this morning. A lot has changed, vanished, or appeared, on the Monterey coast since Vizcaíno and his scurvy-ridden crew drew close to shore that long-ago December day. But some things—the blue bay, the wild and rocky coast, the twisted cypresses and the soft genial climate —have stayed. Monterey, even Vizcaíno would agree, is still a most desirable place.

This anthology is about California's Monterey coast. Not just the eternally haunting aspect of its landscapes and seascapes, but the dramas that were played out against that magnificent backdrop, too. The writers in this collection, from Dana and Stevenson to Steinbeck and Miller, were there, observers and sometimes participants in those dramas—major and minor, tragic and violent, comic and absurd.

For two or three thousand years the native Indians had lived in peace and relative plenty along the Monterey coast. Occasional stops by sixteenth and seventeenth century European mariners did little to disrupt their way of life, and a good life it seems to have been, in close harmony with land and sea. But when the first organized vanguard of Civilization, a small band of Spanish priests and soldiers, finally arrived in 1770, the natives' life changed quickly. A mission and a fort were established by the light-skinned invaders; the Indians were promptly rounded up, clothed, and herded into mission compounds; and Monterey, by Royal Decree, was named capital of the Spanish colonial outpost known as Alta California.

Settlers came and Monterey grew, first under the Spanish flag; then, after the revolution of 1822, under the banner of Mexico. The crescent bay became an active port of call for ships from round the world— whalers, traders, smugglers, even an occasional pirate vessel. Monterey's white adobe walls and red tile rooftops were a welcome sight to sailors on the Pacific run —"decidedly the pleasantest and most civilized looking place in California," was Richard Henry Dana's appraisal. Like all seaports before or since, Monterey had its share of outcasts, rogues, and ruffians. In 1846, on the eve of the Mexican–American War, the Yankee preacher Walter Colton found the town brimming with unsavory characters: "Here is the reckless Californian, the half-wild Indian, the roving trapper of the west, the lawless Mexican, the licentious Spaniard, the absconding Frenchman, the luckless Irishman, the plodding German, the adventurous Russian, the discontented Mormon. . . ."

Mexico lost California to the United States in 1848, and the following year Monterey welcomed the first state constitutional convention with flags and fandangos. Monterey's hopes of remaining capital of the new state were dashed, however, when the delegates voted to move the government to San Jose. To make matters worse, most of Monterey's able-bodied men were deserting the town for the gold fields, and San Francisco had suddenly become the favored California seaport. Almost overnight Monterey reverted to a sleepy little pueblo, a quiet corner of old California. For three decades it languished, forsaken and almost forgotten.

Then things again began to stir. A railroad arrived, linking the Monterey Peninsula with the outside world, and a new kind of emigrant, the tourist, arrived with it. The sudden influx of fashionable sightseers distressed a young Scots visitor named Robert Louis Stevenson. "Alas for the little town!" he lamented in 1879. "It is not strong enough to resist the flaunting caravanserai, and the poor, quaint, penniless native gentlemen of Monterey must perish, like a lower race, before the millionaire vulgarians of the Big Bonanza." Some of the "vulgarians" shared no such sentiments about old Monterey. "It is dirty, it is dusty," complained one fastidious Englishwoman, "it is utterly devoid of all modern improvements."

Nevertheless, by the turn of the century the tourists business was thriving. The sardine industry was growing by leaps and bounds. Real estate men were carving the Peninsula and its three towns—Monterey, Pacific Grove, and the newly created Carmel-by-the-Sea—into $50 and $100 lots which could sometimes be purchased for as little as $5 down and $5 a month. And in the beautiful Carmel pine forest, where the living was cheap and the inspiration abundant, a group of poets, painters, writers and dreamers were creating a true bohemian colony. Led by the poet George Sterling, the colony flourished from about 1905 to the First World War, numbering among its visitors and residents Jack London, Mary Austin, Sinclair Lewis, and a host of other authors and artists. Many years later, in a eulogy to Sterling, Mary Austin captured the essence of the Carmel life: "We achieved, all of us who flocked there . . . a settled habit of morning work. . . . But by the early

afternoon mail, one and another of the painter and
writer folk could be seen sauntering by the piney trails,
which had not then suffered that metamorphosis of
concrete and carbon monoxide that go in the world of
realtors by the name of 'improvements.' . . . There
would be tea beside driftwood fires, or mussel roasts by
moonlight—or the lot of us would pound abalone for
chowder around the open-air grill at Sterling's cabin.
And talk, ambrosial, unquotable talk!"

Today, a certain metamorphosis of concrete and
carbon monoxide is evident on the Monterey coast. But
is it not everywhere? Nearly 200,000 people make their
homes here. Nearly 5 million people come each year to
visit: to drive the Seventeen Mile Drive, to browse the
quaint shops and galleries of Carmel, to tour the old
adobes and ancient mission, to eat fresh seafood at
Fisherman's Wharf, to experience a Point Lobos sunset. Monterey remains a place like no other on earth.
Let it always remain so. Let it always remain all that
can be desired.

WHEN IT HAPPENED

1542   Juan Rodriguez Cabrillo, a Portuguese naviga-
        tor in service of Spain, sails into the present Bay
        of Monterey, which he names Bahia de los
        Pinos, "Bay of the Pines."

1602   Sebastián Vizcaíno, another Portuguese naviga-
        tor working for Spain, anchors in Monterey Bay
        during an exploratory voyage along the coast of
        California. The following day, he and his crew
        go ashore to celebrate a thanksgiving mass, and
        he names the port "Monterey" in honor of
        Gaspar De Zuniga y Acevedo (Count of Mon-
        terey), Ninth Viceroy of Mexico. Some days
        later Vizcaíno discovers and names the Carmel
        River, in honor of the Carmelite friars ac-
        companying the expedition. Vizcaíno's report to
        the king praises Monterey as an outstanding
        port, but Spain, preoccupied elsewhere, does not
        colonize California until 1769–1770.

1769   Gaspar de Portolá, marching north from San
        Diego with troops in search of the Monterey Bay
        described by Vizcaíno, passes it without rec-
        ognizing it. He returns to San Diego.

1770   Portolá finally reaches Monterey on his second
        expedition. The ship *San Antonio,* carrying
        Father Junípero Serra, reaches Monterey, join-
        ing the Portolá expedition.

        At Monterey Bay Father Serra founds mission

San Carlos Borromeo de Monterey, the second mission to be established in Alta (Upper) California.

1771 Serra, wishing to separate the Indians from the Spanish soldiers, and hoping to find a more fertile location, moves the mission a few miles south to the Carmel River and renames it Mission San Carlos Borromeo del Rio Carmelo— Carmel Mission.

1775 Monterey becomes the provincial capital of California.

1776 Juan Bautista de Anza, leading the first band of California colonists overland from Mexico, reaches Monterey.

1784 Father Serra dies and is buried at Carmel Mission.

1786 Jean François Galaup de la Pérouse, in command of a French scientific expedition, arrives in Monterey. He introduces the potato to California and is highly critical of the mission system under which the Indians are forced to serve.

1791 John Graham arrives and becomes the first American in California. Unfortunately, he dies in Monterey on the day of his arrival, September 13.

1796 The ship *Otter* arrives at Monterey Bay, becoming the first American ship to visit.

1818 The pirate Hippolyte de Bouchard sails into Monterey Bay, captures and sacks the deserted town after the residents flee.

1822 California pledges allegiance to the newly created Mexican Empire.

1825 California formally becomes a territory of the Mexican Republic. Jose Maria Echeandia is sent from Mexico to govern California.

1826 The population of Monterey is estimated at 114

civilians, not counting military personnel and Indians.

1828–1844   California enters a period of successive revolutions, and counter revolutions, most of them bloodless. Monterey sees a succession of governors come and go.

1838   The *Beaver*, first steamship in Pacific waters, enters Carmel Bay.

1842   Thinking the United States is at war with Mexico, Commodore Thomas Ap Catesby Jones seizes Monterey on October 19 and raises the U.S. flag. Two days later he realizes his mistake, withdraws and apologizes.

1846   War breaks out between the United States and Mexico. Commodore John D. Sloat raises the American flag at Monterey on July 7, and declares California a U.S. possession. A number of battles and minor skirmishes take place up and down California. The first issue of the Monterey *Californian* appears. This is Monterey's, and California's, first newspaper.

1847   The final battle between U.S. and California troops takes place near Los Angeles on January 9. On January 13, the Californians capitulate.

1848   The treaty of peace between the U.S. and Mexico is signed and California becomes a U.S. territory. Monterey remains a provisional capital.

1849   A constitutional convention meets in Colton Hall, Monterey, to draft a State constitution which is signed on October 13. The State capital is promptly moved to San Jose and Monterey enters a period of decline.

1854   Whaling operations are organized at Monterey Bay.

1859   The Monterey town council deeds all town lands

not privately owned to D. R. Ashley and David Jacks as settlement of a debt of $1,002.50. The council then discreetly adjourns, not to meet again until 1865.

1860   Monterey's population reaches 1,653.

1875   Pacific Grove is founded as a "Christian Seaside Resort." The town laws forbid liquor and dancing and call for young people to be off the streets by 8 P.M. in winters, 9 P.M. in summers.

1880   The Hotel Del Monte opens, and a new era of tourism begins.

1889   Monterey is incorporated as a city.

1900   Monterey's population is 1,748; Pacific Grove's is 1,411.

1902   The Booth Cannery is founded for the purpose of processing and canning sardines. Monterey subsequently becomes known as "sardine capital of the world."

1904   Carmel begins to attract a number of artists, writers, poets, and assorted "bohemians."

1910   Monterey's population is 4,923; Pacific Grove's is 2,384.

1915   The Seventeen-Mile-Drive is finished and opened to automobile traffic, instantly becoming a worldwide attraction.

1916   Carmel-by-the-Sea is incorporated as a town. Elections pit "progressives" (in favor of paved streets, electric lights, mail deliveries, and growth), against "anti-progressives" who oppose nearly all concessions to modernity. Anti-progressives win and throughout the 1920s Carmel purposely remains "behind the times."

1920   Monterey Peninsula's population is 9,091.

1931   A committee is formed to save, refurbish, and restore many of Monterey's historic buildings.

1937   The Carmel–San Simeon Highway along the
       Pacific Coast south of Monterey is opened.

1940   Monterey Peninsula's population now surpasses
       18,000.

1945– The sardines in Monterey Bay suddenly disap-
1946   pear and the canneries shut down.

1960   Monterey Peninsula's population exceeds 40,-
       000.

1970   Monterey celebrates its bicentennial with ap-
       propriate festivities; Peninsula's population ex-
       ceeds 100,000; 4 million tourists come annually.

NAMES ON THE MONTEREY COAST

BIG SUR: The coastal area south of Monterey near the mouth of the Big Sur River. The name is an English–Spanish hybrid meaning "Big South." The region includes Pfeiffer Big Sur State Park with its stands of redwoods and a spectacular shoreline. Big Sur has long been a mecca for tourists, artists, writers. One of its most famous inhabitants was Henry Miller whose *Big Sur and the Oranges of Hieronymous Bosch* describes his life there during the 1940s.

CARMEL: In December of 1602 the explorer Vizcaíno named the Carmel River in honor of the Carmelite priests who were sailing with him. Carmel Bay, Carmel Mission (full name, Mission San Carlos Borromeo del Carmelo), and the present city of Carmel (originally called Carmel-by-the-Sea) all derive from the original Vizcaíno naming. The city of Carmel began as a quaint little artists' and writers' colony in the early years of the twentieth century.

CASTROVILLE: A town a few miles north of Monterey founded in 1864 by Juan Castro. Located on a fertile coastal plain, Castroville calls itself "Artichoke Capital of the World."

DEL MONTE: The name was first given to the luxury hotel that was built not far from Monterey in 1880.

Inspiration for the name may have come from an early Spanish rancho in the vicinity called De la Puente del Monte—"ranch of the mountain bridge."

GABILAN RANGE: A branch of the Coast Range that lies east of the Monterey Peninsula. The name means "hawk" in Spanish. Some of John Steinbeck's stories were laid there. Gabilan Peak, the highest mountain in the range, is also referred to as Frémont Peak. Capt. John C. Frémont erected a fort here in 1846 as one of the first provocations in the American conquest of California. The peak and surrounding terrain are now a state park.

MONTEREY: The name was given first to the bay by the explorer Vizcaíno in 1602 in honor of his superior Gaspar de Zuniga, Viceroy of New Spain and Count of Monterey. The town of Monterey was established by the Spanish colonizers nearly 170 years later and became California's first capital. Monterey County was created in 1850, shortly after California became a state.

MOSS LANDING: Situated a few miles north of Monterey, the landing was founded by Charles Moss in the 1850s as a coastal shipping and whaling station.

PACIFIC GROVE: The town began in 1875 as Methodist colony and health resort under the leadership of David Jacks who also named it. The community's blue laws gave it a straight-laced reputation that still persists.

POINT LOBOS: A spectacular promontory that juts out to sea at the southern tip of Carmel Bay. Point Lobos was originally Punta de los Lobos Marinos—point of the sea wolves—so named by the Spanish seamen for the seals that inhabited the rocky shoreline.

Robert Louis Stevenson is believed to have modeled Spyglass Hill in *Treasure Island* on Point Lobos. The point also figures in some of the Robinson Jeffers' poems and provides the setting for several incidents in Jack London's *Valley of the Moon.* Point Lobos is now a California state park.

SANTA LUCIA RANGE: A coastal mountain range that begins below Carmel and runs south almost to San Luis Obisbo. The ruggedness of the mountains made any large-scale settlement impossible, and it was not until 1937 that a highway was completed along the coastal side of the range. For most of its length, the Santa Lucia rises steeply up out of the sea. Robinson Jeffers drew upon a number of local tales, legends, and incidents—some of them bloody—for the themes of his longer poems.

A PENINSULA PORTRAIT

Mary Austin

Mary Hunter was a Midwestern girl who came to California in 1888 at the age of twenty. While teaching school in Bakersfield, she met Stafford W. Austin, married him in 1891 and moved to Owens Valley. But her unconventional ideas, her intellectual bent, and her friendship with the Indians and Chinese of the region did not sit well with her rural neighbors, and she left—without her husband—for happier climes. In 1904 she visited San Francisco where she met poet George Sterling and, like him, settled a year or so later in Carmel. These two formed the nucleus of the budding coastal bohemia of writers and artists. In Carmel's pine forest she built a house and next to it erected a tree platform (called the Wick-i-up) where she spent the mornings writing. Austin's life was not altogether a happy one: She was short and homely—self-consciously so. Her marriage had failed and her only child was born retarded. Her personality seems not to have endeared her to acquaintances. Sterling at one point assured Ambrose Bierce, who was planning a Carmel visit, "I will spare you from Mary Austin." Nevertheless, her writing was, and remains, highly regarded. Novels, stories, plays, and articles flowed from her pen, and one critic called her "the only literary voice in California worth listening to." *Land of Little Rain* (1903) is a series of beautifully woven sketches of

1

the arid Owens Valley and regions adjacent. During her Carmel stay she wrote and produced several plays in the local Forest Theatre, which she also helped to found. She died in 1934. The following is excerpted from *California, Land of the Sun*, a travel book published in England in 1914.

We struggle so to achieve a little brief moment of beauty, but every hour at Monterey it is given away.

The bay lies squarely fronting the Pacific swell, about a hundred miles south of the Golden Gate, between the horns of two of the little tumbled coast ranges, cutting back to receive the waters of the Pajaro and the Salinas. From the south the hill juts out sharply, taking the town and the harbour between its knees, but the north shore is blunted by the mountains of Santa Cruz. The beach is narrow, and all along its inner curve blown up into dunes contested every season by the wind and by the quick, bright growth of sand verbena, lupins, and mesembryanthemums. The waters of the rivers are set back by the tides, they are choked with bars and sluiced out by winter floods. For miles back into the valleys of Pajaro and Salinas, blue and yellow lupins continue the colour of the sand and the pools of tide water. They climb up the landward slope of the high dunes and set the shore a little seaward against the diminished surf. Then the equinoctial tide rises against the land that the lupins have taken and smooths out their lovely gardens with a swift, white hand, to leave the beach smooth again for the building of pale, wind-pointed cones.

A windy bay at best, deep tides, and squally surfaces, the waters of Monterey have other values than the colourist finds in them. Sardines, salmon, cod, tuna, yellow tail run with its tides. At most seasons of the year whales may be seen spouting there, or are cast upon its shoals. At one time the port enjoyed a certain prosperity as a whaling station, of which small trace remains beside the bleaching vertebrae that border certain of the old gardens and the persistent whalebone souvenirs of the curio dealer. Lateen-rigged fisher fleets flock in and out of the harbour, butterfly winged; and all about the rock beaches creep the square-toed boats of the Japanese and Chinese abalone gatherers. Thousands of purple sea-urchins, squid, hundred-fingered star-fish, and all manner of slimy sea delicacies, these slant-eyed Orientals draw up out of the rainbow rock pools and the deeps below the receding surf. They go creeping and peering about the ebb, their guttural hunting cries borne inshore on the quiet air, seeming as much a native sea speech as the gabble of the gulls. So in their skin canoes and balsas the Indians must have crept about the inlets.

Other and less fortunate adventurers on the waters of Monterey have left strange traces on that coast; one stumbles on a signboard set up among the rocks to mark where such and such a vessel went to pieces in a night of storm. Buried deep in the beach beyond the anchorage is the ancient teakwood hull of the *Natala,* the ship that carried Napoleon to Elba. It brought secularisation to the Missions also, after which unfriendly service the wind woke in the night and broke it against the shore. Just off Point Lobos, the Japanese divers after abalones report a strange, uncharted, sunken craft, a Chinese junk blown out of her course perhaps, or one of those unreported galleons that followed a phantom trail of gold all up the west coast of the New World. Strange mosses come ashore here, tide by tide, all lacy and scarf-coloured, and once we found on the tiny strand below Pescadero, a log of sandal-

wood with faint waterworn traces of tool marks still
upon it.

Across the neck of the peninsula, a matter of six or
eight miles, cuts in the little bay of Carmel, a blue
jewel set in silver sand. Two points divide it from the
racing Pacific, the southern limb of Punta [Point] Pinos,
and the deeply divided rocky ledge of Point Lobos—
Lobos, the wolf, with thin, raking, granite jaws. Now
on these two points, and nowhere else in the world, are
found natural plantations of the trees that might have
grown in Dante's Purgatorio, or in the imagined forests
where walked the rapt, tormented soul of Blake. Blake,
indeed, might have had a hint of these from some
transplanted seedling on an English terrace, for the
Monterey cypress is quick-growing for the first century
or so and one of the most widely diffused of trees; but
only here on the Point and south to Pescadero ranch do
they grow of God's planting. With writhen trunks and
stiff contorted limbs they take the storm and flying
scud as poppies take the sun.

Three little towns have taken root on the Peninsula:
two on the bay side, the old pueblo of Monterey with
its white-washed adobes still contriving to give character to the one wide street; and Pacific Grove, utterly modern, on the surf side of Punta de Pinos, a town
which began, I believe, as a resort for the churchly
minded—a very clean and well-kept and proper town,
absolutely exempt, as the deeds are drawn to assure us,
"from anything having a tendency to lower the moral
atmosphere," a town where the lovely natural woods
have given place to houses every fifty feet or so, all
nicely soldered together with lines of bright scarlet and
clashing magentas and rosy pinks of geraniums and
pelargoniums in a kind of predetermined cheerfulness;

in short, a town where nobody would think of living who wanted anything interesting to happen to him.

The modern Carmel is a place of resort for painter and poet folk. Beauty is cheap there; it may be had in superlative quality for the mere labour of looking out of the window. It is the absolute setting for romance. No shipping ever puts in at the singing beaches. The freighting teams from the Sur with their bells a-jangle, go by on the country road, but great dreams have visited the inhabitants thereof. Spring visits it also with yellow violets all up the wooded hills, and great fountain sprays of sea-blue ceanothus. Summer reddens the berries of the manzanita and mellows the poppy-blazoned slopes to tawny saffron. Strong tides arrive unheralded from some far-off deep-sea disturbance and shake the beaches. Suddenly, on the quietest days, some flying squadron of the deep breaks high over Lobos and neighs in her narrow caverns. Blown foam, whipped all across the Pacific, is cast up like weed along the sand and skims the wave-marks with a winged motion. Whole flocks of these foam-birds may be seen scudding toward the rock-corners of Mission Point after the equinoctial winds. In other tides the sea slips far out on new-made level reaches, and leaves the wet sand shining after the sun goes down like the rosy inside pearl of the abalone.

TRADING DAYS AT MONTEREY

Richard Henry Dana

On a "fine Saturday afternoon" in January, 1835, a Boston sailing ship dropped anchor in Monterey Bay and a young seaman named Richard Henry Dana got his first glimpse of the capital of Alta California. For the nineteen-year-old Dana, the white-washed houses and red tile roofs of Monterey were an agreeable sight, a distinct improvement over the "little dark looking town" of Santa Barbara to the south. Dana was no ordinary seaman. The son of an old and prominent New England family, he had five months earlier decided to trade the uniform of a Harvard undergraduate for the dress of a "dog before the mast." It was a voyage that would take him from Boston, down the coast of South America, around the Horn, and up to Mexican California where a year would be spent cruising and trading, then back to Boston. Dana's account of the voyage, from which the following selection is taken, appeared in 1840 as *Two Years Before the Mast*. Dana saw California at the height of the "hide and tallow era," a time of brisk commerce between New England trading vessels and the California cattle ranchers. His *Two Years Before the Mast* has been termed by critic Lawrence Clark Powell as "the first, and it remains the greatest, book of marine California." Following his return to Boston, Dana re-entered Harvard, took up the law, and became a strong champion of unpopular causes, including seamen's rights and the

abolition of slavery. He died in Rome at the age of
sixty-six.

━━━━━━━━━━━━━◄◄►◄◄◄◄►◄►━━━━━━━━━━━━━

The bay of Monterey is wide at the entrance, being
about twenty-four miles between the two points, Año
Nuevo at the north, and Pinos at the south, but nar-
rows gradually as you approach the town, which is
situated in a bend, or large cove, at the south-eastern
extremity, and from the points about eighteen miles,
which is the whole depth of the bay. The shores are
extremely well wooded (the pine abounding upon
them), and as it was now the rainy season, everything
was as green as nature could make it—the grass, the
leaves, and all; the birds were singing in the woods, and
great numbers of wild fowl were flying over our heads.
Here we could lie safe from the south-easters. We came
to anchor within two cables' lengths of the shore, and
the town lay directly before us, making a very pretty
appearance, its houses being of white-washed adobe,
which gives a much better effect than those of Santa
Barbara, which are mostly left of a mud colour. The
red tiles too, on the roofs, contrasted well with the
white sides and with the extreme greenness of the lawn,
upon which the houses—about a hundred in number
—were dotted about, here and there, irregularly. There
are in this place, and in every other town which I saw
in California, no streets nor fences (except that here
and there a small patch might be fenced in for a garden), so that the houses are placed at random upon
the green. This, as they are of one story, and of the
cottage form, gives them a pretty effect when seen from
a little distance.

It was a fine Saturday afternoon that we came to
anchor, the sun about an hour high, and everything
looking pleasant. The Mexican flag was flying from the

little square presidio, and the drums and trumpets of the soldiers, who were out on parade, sounded over the water, and gave great life to the scene. Every one was delighted with the appearance of things. We felt as though we had got into a Christian (which in the sailor's vocabulary means civilised) country.

The next day being Sunday, which is the liberty-day among merchantmen, when it is usual to let a part of the crew go ashore, the sailors had depended upon a holiday, and were already disputing who should ask to go, when, upon being called in the morning, we were turned-to upon the rigging, and found that the topmast, which had been sprung, was to come down, and a new one to go up, with topgallant and royal masts, and the rigging to be set. This was too bad. If there is anything that irritates sailors, and makes them feel hardly used, it is being deprived of their Sunday. Not that they would always, or indeed generally, spend it improvingly, but it is their only day of rest. Then, too, they are so often necessarily deprived of it by storms and unavoidable duties of all kinds, that to take it from them when lying quietly and safely in port, without any urgent reason, bears the more hardly. The only reason in this case was, that the captain had determined to have the custom-house officers on board on Monday, and wished to have his brig in order. Jack is a slave aboard ship; but still he has many opportunities of thwarting and balking his master. When there is danger or necessity, or when he is well used, no one can work faster than he; but the instant he feels that he is kept at work for nothing, or, as the nautical phrase is, "humbugged," no sloth could make less headway. He must not refuse his duty, or be in any way disobedient, but all the work that an officer gets out of him he may be welcome to. Every man who has been three months

at sea knows how to "work Tom Cox's traverse"—
"three turns round the longboat, and a pull at the
scuttled butt." This morning everything went in this
way. "*Sogering*" was the order of the day. Send a man
below to get a block, and he would capsize everything
before finding it, then not bring it up till an officer
had called him twice, and take as much time to put
things in order again. Marline-spikes were not to be
found; knives wanted a prodigious deal of sharpening,
and generally three or four were waiting round the
grindstone at a time. When a man got to the mast-head,
he would come slowly down again for something he
had left; and after the tackles were got up, six men
would pull less than three who pulled "with a will."
When the mate was out of sight, nothing was done. It
was all up-hill work; and at eight o'clock, when we
went to breakfast, things were nearly where they were
when we began.

During our short meal the matter was discussed. One
proposed refusing to work; but that was mutiny,
and of course was rejected at once. I remember, too,
that one of the men quoted "Father Taylor" (as they
call the seamen's preacher at Boston), who told them
that, if they were ordered to work on Sunday they
must not refuse their duty, and the blame would not
come upon them. After breakfast it leaked out, through
the officers, that, if we would get through work soon,
we might have a boat in the afternoon and go a-fishing.
This bait was well thrown, and took with several who
were fond of fishing; and all began to find that as we
had one thing to do, and were not to be kept at work
for the day, the sooner we did it the better. Accordingly, things took a new aspect; and before two o'clock,
this work, which was in a fair way to last two days,
was done; and five of us went a-fishing in the jolly-
boat, in the direction of Point Pinos; but leave to go

ashore was refused. Here we saw the *Loriotte,* which sailed with us from Santa Barbara, coming slowly in with a light sea-breeze, which sets in towards afternoon, having been becalmed off the point all the first part of the day. We took several fish of various kinds, among which cod and perch abounded, and Foster (the *ci-devant* second mate), who was of our number, brought up with his hook a large and beautiful pearl-oyster shell. We afterwards learned that this place was celebrated for shells, and that a small schooner had made a good voyage by carrying a cargo of them to the United States.

We returned by sundown, and found the *Loriotte* at anchor within a cable's length of the *Pilgrim.* The next day we were "turned-to" early, and began taking off the hatches, overhauling the cargo, and getting everything ready for inspection. At eight, the officers of the customs, five in number, came on board, and began examining the cargo, manifest, etc. The Mexican revenue laws are very strict, and require the whole cargo to be landed, examined, and taken on board again; but our agent had suceeded in compounding for the last two vessels, and saving the trouble of taking the cargo ashore. The officers were dressed in the costume which we found prevailed through the country— broad-brimmed hat, usually of a black or dark brown colour, with a gilt or figured band round the crown, and lined under the rim with silk; a short jacket of silk or figured calico (the European skirted body-coat is never worn); the shirt open in the neck; rich waistcoat, if any; pantaloons, open at the sides below the knees, laced with gilt, usually of velveteen or broadcloth; or else short breeches and white stockings. They wear the deer-skin shoe, which is of a dark brown colour, and (being made by Indians) usually a good deal ornamented. They have no suspenders, but always wear a sash round the waist, which is generally red, and varying in quality with the means of the wearer. Add to this the never-failing poncho, or the serape, and you have the dress of the Californian. This last garment is always a mark of the rank and wealth of the owner. The *gente de razon,* or better sort of people, wear cloaks of black or dark blue broadcloth with as much velvet and trimmings as may be; and from this they go down to the blanket of the Indian, the middle classes wearing a poncho, something like a large square cloth, with a hole in the middle for the head to go through. This is often as coarse as a blanket, but being beautifully woven with various colours, is quite showy at a distance. Among the Mexicans there is no working class (the Indians being practically serfs, and doing all the hard work); and every rich man looks like a grandee, and every poor scamp like a broken-down gentleman. I have often seen a man, with a fine figure and courteous manners, dressed in broadcloth and velvet, with a noble horse completely covered with trappings, without a *real* in his pockets, and absolutely suffering for something to eat.

The next day, the cargo having been entered in due form, we began trading. The trade-room was fitted up in the steerage, and furnished out with the lighter goods, and with specimens of the rest of the cargo; and Mellus, a young man who came out from Boston with us before the mast, was taken out of the forecastle, and made supercargo's clerk. He was well qualified for this business, having been clerk in a counting-house in Boston; he had been troubled for some time with rheumatism, which unfitted him for the wet and exposed duty of a sailor on the coast. For a week or ten days all was life on board. The people came off to look and to buy—men, women, and children; and we were continually going in the boats, carrying goods and passengers—for they have no boats of their own. Everything must dress itself and come aboard and see the new vessel, if it were only to buy a paper of pins. The agent and his clerk managed the sales, while we were busy in the hold or in the boats. Our cargo was an assorted one; that is, it consisted of everything under the sun. We had spirits of all kinds (sold by the cask), teas, coffee, sugar, spices, raisins, molasses, hardware, crockery-ware, tin-ware, cutlery, clothing of all kinds, boots and shoes from Lynn, calicoes and cottons from Lowell, crapes, silks; also, shawls, scarfs, necklaces, jewelry, and combs for the women; furniture; and, in fact, everything that can be imagined, from Chinese fireworks to English cart-wheels—of which we had a dozen pairs with their iron tires on.

The Californians are an idle, thriftless people, and can make nothing for themselves. The country abounds in grapes, yet they buy, at a great price, bad wine made in Boston and brought round by us, and retail it among themselves at a *real* (12½ cents) by the small wine-glass. Their hides, too, which they value at two dollars in money, they barter for something which costs seventy-five cents in Boston; and buy shoes (as like as not made of their own hides, which have been carried twice round Cape Horn) at three and four dollars, and "chicken-skin boots" at fifteen dollars a pair. Things sell, on an average, at an advance of nearly three hundred per cent. upon the Boston prices. This is partly owing to the heavy duties which the government, in their wisdom, with an idea, no doubt, of keeping the silver in the country, has laid upon imports. These duties, and the enormous expenses of so long a voyage, keep all merchants but those of heavy capital from engaging in the trade.

This kind of business was new to us, and we liked it

very well for a few days, though we were hard at work
every minute from daylight to dark, and sometimes
even later.

By being thus continually engaged in transporting
passengers with their goods, to and fro, we gained considerable knowledge of the character, dress, and language of the people. The dress of the men was as I
have before described it. The women wore gowns of
various texture—silks, crape, calicoes, etc.—made after the European style, except that the sleeves were
short, leaving the arm bare, and that they were loose
about the waist, corsets not being in use. They wore
shoes of kid or satin, sashes or belts of bright colours,
and almost always a necklace and earrings. Bonnets
they had none. I only saw one on the coast, and that
belonged to the wife of an American sea-captain who
had settled in San Diego, and had imported the cha-
otic mass of straw and ribbon as a choice present to
his new wife. They wear their hair (which is almost
invariably black, or a very dark brown) long in their
necks, sometimes loose, and sometimes in long braids;
though the married women often do it up on a high
comb. Their only protection against the sun and weather is a large mantle, which they put over their heads,
drawing it close round their faces when they go out of
doors, which is generally only in pleasant weather.
When in the house or sitting out in front of it, which
they often do in fine weather, they usually wear a small
scarf or neckerchief of a rich pattern. A band, also,
about the top of the head, with a cross, star, or other
ornament in front, is common. Their complexions are
various, depending—as well as their dress and manner—upon the amount of Spanish blood they can lay
claim to, which also settles their social rank. Those
who are of pure Spanish blood, having never inter-
married with the aborigines, have clear brunette com-

plexions, and sometimes even as fair as those of English women. There are but few of these families in California, being mostly those in official stations, or who, on the expiration of their terms of office, have settled here upon property they have acquired; and others who have been banished for state offences. These form the upper class, intermarrying, and keeping up an exclusive system in every respect. They can be distinguished, not only by their complexion, dress, and manners, but also by their speech; for, calling themselves Castilians, they are very ambitious of speaking the pure Castilian, while all Spanish is spoken in a somewhat corrupted dialect by the lower classes. From this upper class they go down by regular shades, growing more and more dark and muddy, until you come to the pure Indian, who runs about with nothing upon him but a small piece of cloth, kept up by a wide leather strap drawn round his waist. Generally speaking, each person's caste is decided by the quality of the blood, which shows itself, too plainly to be concealed, at first sight. Yet the least drop of Spanish blood, if it be only of quadroon or octoroon, is sufficient to raise one from the position of a serf, and entitle him to wear a suit of clothes—boots, hat, cloak, spurs, long knife, all complete, though coarse and dirty as may be—and to call himself Español, and to hold property, if he can get any.

The fondness for dress among the women is excessive, and is sometimes their ruin. A present of a fine mantle, or of a necklace or pair of earrings gains the favour of the greater part. Nothing is more common than to see a woman living in a house of only two rooms, with the ground for a floor, dressed in spangled satin shoes, silk gown, high comb, and gilt, if not gold, earrings and necklace. If their husbands do not dress them well enough, they will soon receive presents from others. They used to spend whole days on board our vessel, examining the fine clothes and ornaments, and frequently making purchases at a rate which would have made a seamstress or waiting-maid in Boston open her eyes.

Next to the love of dress, I was most struck with the fineness of the voices and beauty of the intonations of both sexes. Every common ruffian-looking fellow, with a slouched hat, blanket cloak, dirty under-dress, and soiled leather leggings, appeared to me to be speaking elegant Spanish. It was a pleasure simply to listen to the sound of the language, before I could attach any meaning to it. They have a good deal of the Creole drawl, but it is varied by an occasional extreme rapidity of utterance in which they seem to skip from consonant to consonant, until, lighting upon a broad, open vowel, they rest upon that to restore the balance of sound. The women carry this peculiarity of speaking to a much greater extreme than the men, who have more evenness and stateliness of utterance. A common bullock-driver, on horseback, delivering a message, seemed to speak like an ambassador at a royal audience. In fact, they sometimes appeared to me to be a people on whom a curse had fallen, and stripped them of everything but their pride, their manners, and their voices.

Another thing that surprised me was the quantity of silver in circulation. I never, in my life, saw so much silver at one time as during the week that we were at Monterey. The truth is, they have no credit system, no banks, and no way of investing money but in cattle. Besides silver, they have no circulating medium but hides, which the sailors call "California banknotes." Everything that they buy they must pay for in one or the other of these means.

I had not studied Spanish at college, and could

not speak a word when at Juan Fernandez; but, during the latter part of the passage out, I borrowed a grammar and dictionary from the cabin, and by a continual use of these, and a careful attention to every word that I heard spoken, I soon got a vocabulary together and began talking for myself. As I soon knew more Spanish than any of the crew (who, indeed, knew none at all), and had studied Latin and French, I got the name of a great linguist, and was always sent by the captain and officers for provisions, or to take letters and messages to different parts of the town. I was often sent for something which I could not tell the name of to save my life; but I liked the business, and accordingly never pleaded ignorance. Sometimes I managed to jump below and take a look at my dictionary before going ashore; or else I overhauled some English resident on my way, and learned the word from him; and then, by signs, and by giving a Latin or French word a twist at the end, contrived to get along. This was a good exercise for me, and no doubt taught me more than I should have learned by months of study and reading; it also gave me opportunities of seeing the customs, characters, and domestic arrangements of the people, besides being a great relief from the monotony of a day spent on board ship.

Monterey, as far as my observation goes, is decidedly the pleasantest and most civilised-looking place in California. In the centre of it is an open square, surrounded by four lines of one-story buildings, with half a dozen cannons in the centre; some mounted, and others not. This is the presidio, or fort. Every town has a presidio in its centre, or rather every presidio has a town built around it; for the forts were first built by the Mexican government, and then the people built near them for protection. The presidio here was entirely open and unfortified. There were several officers with long titles, and about eighty soldiers, but they were poorly paid, fed, clothed, and disciplined. The governor-general, or, as he is commonly called, the "general," lives here, which makes it the seat of government. . . . No Protestant has any political rights, nor can he hold property, or, indeed, remain more than a few weeks on shore, unless he belong to a foreign vessel. Consequently, Americans and English, who intend to reside here, become Papists—the current phrase among them being, "A man must leave his conscience at Cape Horn."

But, to return to Monterey. The houses here, as everywhere else in California, are of one story, built of *adobes*, that is, clay made into large bricks, about a foot and a half square, and three or four inches thick, and hardened in the sun. These are joined together by a cement of the same material, and the whole are of a common dirt colour. The floors are generally of earth, the windows grated and without glass; and the doors, which are seldom shut, open directly into the common room, there being no entries. Some of the more wealthy inhabitants have glass to their windows, and board floors; and in Monterey nearly all the houses are white-washed on the outside. The better houses, too, have red tiles upon the roofs. The common ones have two or three rooms, which open into each other, and are furnished with a bed or two, a few chairs and tables, a looking-glass, a crucifix, and small daubs of paintings enclosed in glass, representing some miracle or martyrdom. They have no chimneys or fireplaces in the houses, the climate being such as to make a fire unnecessary; and all their cooking is done in a small kitchen, separated from the house. The Indians, as I have said before, do all the hard work, two or three being attached to the better house; and the poorest persons are able to keep one at least; for they have only to feed them, and give them a small piece of coarse cloth and a belt for the men, and a coarse gown, without shoes or stockings, for the women.

In Monterey there are a number of English and Americans (English or Inglés all are called who speak the English language) who have married Californians, become united to the Roman Church, and acquired considerable property. Having more industry, frugality, and enterprise than the natives, they soon get nearly all the trade into their hands. They usually keep shops, in which they retail the goods purchased in larger quantities from our vessels, and also send a good deal into the interior, taking hides in pay, which they again barter with our ships. In every town on the coast there are foreigners engaged in this kind of trade, while I recollect but two shops kept by natives. The people are naturally suspicious of foreigners, and they would not be allowed to remain, were it not that they conform to the Church; and by marrying natives, and bringing up their children as Roman Catholics and Mexicans, and not teaching them the English language, they quiet suspicion, and even become popular and leading men. The chief alcaldes in Monterey and Santa Barbara were Yankees by birth.

The men in Monterey appeared to me to be always on horseback. Horses are as abundant here as dogs and chickens were in Juan Fernandez. There are no stables to keep them in, but they are allowed to run wild and graze wherever they please, being branded, and having long leather ropes, called lassos, attached to their necks and dragging along behind them, by which they can be easily taken. The men usually catch one in the morning, throw a saddle and bridle upon him, and use him for the day, and let him go at night, catching another the next day. When they go on long journeys, they ride one horse down and catch another, throw the saddle and bridle upon him, and after riding him down take a third, and so on to the end of the journey. There are probably no better riders in the world. They are put upon a horse when only four or five years old, their little legs not long enough to come half-way over his sides, and may almost be said to keep on him until they have grown to him. The stirrups are covered or boxed up in front, to prevent their catching when riding through the woods; and the saddles are large and heavy, strapped very tight upon the horse, and have large pommels, or loggerheads, in front, round which the lasso is coiled when not in use. They can hardly go from one house to another without mounting a horse, there being generally several standing tied to the doorposts of the little cottages. When they wish to show their activity, they make no use of their stirrups in mounting, but striking the horse, spring into the saddle as he starts, and sticking their long spurs into him, go off on the full run. Their spurs are cruel things, having four or five rowels, each an inch in length, dull and rusty. The flanks of the horses are often sore from them, and I have seen men come in from chasing bullocks with their horses' hind legs and quarters covered with blood. They frequently give exhibitions of their horsemanship in races, bull-baitings, etc.; but as we were not ashore during any holiday, we saw nothing of it. Monterey is also a great place for cock-fighting, gambling of all sorts, fandangos, and various kinds of amusement and knavery. Trappers and hunters, who occasionally arrive here from over the Rocky Mountains, with their valuable skins and furs, are often entertained with amusements and dissipation, until they have wasted their opportunities and their money, and then go back, stripped of everything.

Nothing but the character of the people prevents Monterey from becoming a large town. The soil is as rich as man could wish, climate as good as any in the world, water abundant, and situation extremely beautiful. The harbour, too, is a good one, being subject only to one bad wind, the north; and though the holding-ground is not the best, yet I heard of but one vessel being driven ashore here. That was a Mexican brig, which went ashore a few months before our arrival, and was a total wreck, all the crew but one being drowned. Yet this was owing to the carelessness or ignorance of the captain, who paid out all his small cable before he let go his other anchor. The ship *Lagoda* of Boston was there at the time, and rode out the gale in safety, without dragging at all, or finding it necesary to strike the topgallant masts.

Sunday came again while we were at Monterey; but, as before, it brought us no holiday. The people on shore dressed and came off in greater numbers than ever, and we were employed all day in boating and breaking out cargo, so that we had hardly time to eat. Our former second mate, who was determined to get liberty if it was to be had, dressed himself in a long coat and black hat, and polished his shoes, and went aft, and asked to go ashore. He could not have done a more imprudent thing; for he knew that no liberty would be given; and besides, sailors, however sure they may be of having liberty granted them, always go aft in their working clothes, to appear as though they had no reason to expect anything, and then wash, dress, and shave after the matter is settled. But this poor fellow was always getting into hot water, and if there was a wrong way of doing a thing, was sure to hit upon it. We looked to see him go aft, knowing pretty well what his reception would be. The captain was walking the quarter-deck, smoking his morning cigar, and Foster went as far as the break of the deck, and there waited for him to notice him. The captain took two or three turns, and then, walking directly up to him, surveyed him from head to foot, and lifting up his forefinger, said a word or two, in a tone too low for us to hear, but which had a magical effect upon poor Foster. He walked forward, jumped down into the forecastle, and in a moment more made his appearance in his common clothes, and went quietly to work again. What the captain said to him, we never could get him to tell, but it certainly changed him outwardly and inwardly in a surprising manner.

After a few days, finding the trade beginning to slacken, we hove our anchor up, set our topsails, ran the stars and stripes up to the peak, fired a gun, which was returned from the presidio, and left the little town astern, standing out of the bay, and bearing down the coast again for Santa Barbara. . . . [Eleven months passed before Dana saw Monterey again.]

At midnight, the tide having turned, we hove up our anchor and stood out of the bay [of San Francisco], with a fine starry heaven above us—the first we had seen for many weeks. Before the light northerly winds, which blow here with the regularity of trades, we worked slowly along, and made Point Año Nuevo, the northerly point of the Bay of Monterey, on Monday afternoon. We spoke, going in, the brig *Diana,* of the Sandwich Islands, from the North-west Coast, last from Sitka. She was off the point at the same time with us, but did not get in to the anchoring-ground until an hour or two after us. It was ten o'clock on Tuesday morning when we came to anchor. Monterey looked just as it did when I saw it last, which was eleven months before. . . . The pretty lawn on which it stands, as green as sun and rain could make it; the pine wood on the south; the small river on the north side; the adobe houses, with their white walls and red-tiled roofs, dotted about on the green; the low, white presidio with its soiled tri-coloured flag flying, and the discordant din of drums and trumpets of the noon parade—all brought up the scene we had witnessed here with so much pleasure nearly a year before, when coming from a long voyage, and from our unprepossessing reception at Santa Barbara. It seemed almost like coming to a home.

As we were to be here over Sunday, and Monterey was the best place to go ashore on the whole coast, and we had had no liberty-day for nearly three months, every one was for going ashore. On Sunday morning as soon as the decks were washed, and we were through breakfast, those who had obtained liberty began to clean themselves, as it is called, to go ashore. Buckets of fresh water, cakes of soap, large coarse towels, and we went to work scrubbing one another on the forecastle. Having gone through this, the next thing was to step into the head—one on each side—with a bucket apiece, and duck one another, by drawing up water and heaving over each other, while we were stripped to a pair of trousers. Then came the rigging-up. The usual outfit of pumps, white stockings, loose white duck trousers, blue jackets, clean checked shirts, black kerchiefs, hats well varnished, with a fathom of black ribbon over the left eye, a silk handkerchief flying from the outside jacket pocket, and four or five dollars tied up in the back of the neckerchief, and we were "all right." One of the quarter-boats pulled us ashore, and we streamed up to the town. I tried to find the church, in order to see the worship, but was told that there was no service, except a mass early in the morning; so we went about the town, visiting the Americans and English, and the Mexicans whom we had known when we were here before. Toward noon we procured horses, and rode out to the Carmel Mission, which is about a league from the town, where we got something in the way of a dinner—beef, eggs, frijoles, tortillas, and some middling wine—from the major-domo, who, of course, refused to make any charge, as it was the Lord's gift, yet received our present, as a gratuity, with a low bow, a touch of the hat, and "Dios se lo pague!"

After this repast we had a fine run, scouring the country on our fleet horses, and came into town soon after sundown. Here we found our companions, who had refused to go to ride with us, thinking that a sailor has no more business with a horse than a fish has with a balloon. They were moored, stem and stern, in a grog-shop, making a great noise, with a crowd of Indians and hungry half-breeds about them, and with a fair prospect of being stripped and dirked, or left to pass the night in the calabozo. With a great deal of trouble we managed to get them down to the boats, though not without many angry looks and interferences from the Mexicans, who had marked them out for their prey. The *Diana's* crew—a set of worthless outcasts, who had been picked up at the islands from the refuse of whale-ships—were all as drunk as beasts, and had a set-to on the beach with their captain, who was in no better state than themselves. They swore they would not go aboard, and went back to the town, were robbed and beaten, and lodged in the calabozo until the next day, when the captain brought them out. Our forecastle, as usual after a liberty-day, was a scene of tumult all night long, from the drunken ones. They had just got to sleep towards morning when they were turned-up with the rest, and kept at work all day in the water, carrying hides, their heads aching so that they could hardly stand. This is sailors' pleasure.

MANNERS, MORALS, AND MURDERS

Dr. R. T. Maxwell

For an outsider visiting Monterey in 1842, life could be dangerous—and full of surprises. Young Dr. Maxwell was assistant surgeon on the frigate *United States*, commanded by Commodore Thomas Ap Catesby Jones. While the vessel was in Peruvian waters, Jones somehow became convinced that Mexico and the U.S. had declared war. Jones sailed immediately for Monterey and took possession of the town only to learn, two days later, that there was no conflict. The incident, since known as "Commodore Jones's War," did nothing to improve the already tense state of affairs between the two countries. Maxwell's account of his experiences was dictated many years after his voyage. The manuscript lay unpublished for many years in the Bancroft Library at Berkeley. In 1955 it was edited by John Haskell Kemble and published as *Visit to Monterey in 1842*, from which the following selection is excerpted.

———— ◆◆ ◆ ◆◆ ————

I was in Monterey from October 1842 to the end of January 1843. We were about twenty five or thirty days on the trip to the Sandwich Islands. We were about three days in possession of the fort. We soon

25

became intimate with many of the families in town, and used to spend our time pleasantly there. But the Californians were very bitter, Castro especially. I remember going with a young man named Gamble to shoot. I bought a fine mare for $9.00. It was considered very ultra for a man to ride a mare in those days, and the girls used to call out after me, "Yegua, yegua,"—meaning a mare. There was a brother of Captain Eagle of the navy who had gone round Cape Horn on a sea voyage for his health, and arrived in California. He was there at the time we were, having come from the Sandwich Islands to Monterey, and had purchased a grey mare which he valued very highly, and when he left, he sold it to me for nine dollars. Hartstene had also bought a horse. He and I were the chief sportsmen of the ship. Game was so abundant that you could knock the ducks down with an oar, and they had never had a gun fired at them.

We used to go ashore hunting, and over to the old Mission, and get an old woman to make tortillas, corn cake, from meal produced by rubbing down between two stones, and she would stew our quail with red peppers, and in that way we got our dinner. We chanced to go to the Mission of Carmel, on the feast of San Juan, and we found Castro with some twenty half drunken Indians, and among them we found also Padre Real, the priest of Monterey, who afterward was, with Larkin, one of the original [discoverers] of the Almaden quicksilver mine, Larkin having tested the ore in a gun barrel. Father Real requested me to dress the wound of an Indian boy, whose foot had been mashed by a mule. I amputated his toe with my pocket knife. I had with me a negro boy with a Colt's rifle, thinking we might meet bears, as we saw their tracks and excrements in the woods. I played some waltzes on a fiddle with two silk strings, and one of catgut and one of wire, for the Indian women to dance. Of course, I was quite popular at the moment; they considered my playing a great thing. Father Real called me to one side, and cautioned me not to leave his side while we were there, as Castro, who was a very brutal man, and half drunk, was inciting the Indians to kill us. He most particularly cautioned me not to let him get hold of this rifle, which he was anxious to obtain. He had never seen anything of the kind in the country; there were two chambers of five barrels each, good for ten shots. We kept near him, and he went with us to the outside of the wall, Castro thinking we were still visiting the sick Indian boy, when we mounted our horses and left the road, and went across the mountain to Point Pinos, finding our way by the sound of the sea. When we looked back, we saw these Indians chasing along, as we supposed in pursuit of us, Castro at their head. We got aboard the ship about 11 o'clock at night, in a boat from the shore, and I reported the matter to Captain Armstrong, who sent an officer the next day to demand that Castro should be called to account for it. He made many apologies, and attributed his conduct to his having been drunk at the time, and at the ball at the Government House which we gave them on New Year's evening, he made what he considered ample amends to me by embracing me and kissing me on each cheek. If it had not been for the priest we would have been killed that day. When the Bishop came here, he ordered him off to the middle of Mexico somewhere; the old fellow's morals were not very good.

On the night of the First of January, we gave them a ball at the Government House. At that time, the female population of Monterey had never tasted cake, mince pie, or anything of that sort. The Stewards of

our messes were set to work making all kinds of delicacies in the shape of cakes and pies for the supper
at the ball. Our wine from Madeira was all expended,
so we were obliged to depend on whisky toddy, which
the ladies thought was very fine, and indulged in rather too freely, some of them. . . . These people had
the most extraordinary customs. They came on board
the ship and danced all day, and we would go on
shore and dance all night. They would sit down to
the table, and every woman would spread her handkerchief on her lap, and whatever we had on the table
they would eat a part of, and carry off a part in their
handkerchiefs,—nuts, figs, everything. Their manners
were exceedingly primitive. There were three very pretty girls who were nieces of Capt. Cooper's wife, and
they were great belles. I took charge of one of them
in going to the ball. They were dressed in thin muslin.
As we passed along the street, she said "Excuse me
for a moment," and sat down by the fence, and dis-
charged the contents of her bladder. There were a
couple of midshipmen behind us at the time. These
women were as unsophisticated as so many cats.

There was an old fellow here, just as Gamble came,
who was collecting natural curiosities for some of the
German princes. I was sent for to go out from Monterey, some twenty or twenty two miles toward Hart-
nell's ranch. I went, with a couple of men, and found
that this man had been shot through the lung by an
Indian arrow. Some of the Diggers had attacked him in
the woods. It was necessary to push the arrow through,
and cut it off, and then draw it back, in order to get
it out.

When I was at the Carmel Mission back of Monterey,
the Church was in tolerable repair. There were a number of curious paintings there, and among them one of
the Landing of Vancouver, a picture about seven feet

by eleven, painted chiefly with chrome earth found here, and probably done by one of the ship's painters from his vessel. They presented it to this church. There were twenty one paintings about eight by twelve, representing Heaven and Hell. Hell was represented by the old mythological characters, while Heaven was represented as a ball room, with angels and other figures dancing and playing the guitar and tambourine. These were used to convert the Indians. There were some smaller paintings, some of them really beautiful, one of them representing St. John. I, seeing that everything was going to ruin, went to Father Real, and asked him if I could purchase any of these pictures. He said that he could not sell anything belonging to the church, but he could not tell whether there were six or sixty pictures; in other words, he was telling me to go and help myself, and not let him know it. I did not like to do that, however, as an officer of the squadron. What became of these pictures I do not know.

The morals of the people were pretty good. One of the great belles, the prettiest woman in the place, was a cousin of Don Pablo de la Guerra, or some relative of his, and her hatred of the Americans was so great that she promised to marry anybody who would bring her a necklace made of their ears. She wound up, however, by marrying an American.

MONTEREY IN '46

Walter Colton

Walter Colton (1797–1851) was Monterey's first American *alcalde* or mayor, having been given the job in 1846, following the outbreak of war with Mexico and the seizure of California by Commodore John D. Sloat. Colton was a New England minister who had come to California as a Navy chaplain. The job of *alcalde* was no easy task, embracing many duties, as Colton himself noted: "every breach of peace, every case of crime, every business obligation and every disputed land title." The minister turned mayor performed these duties ably and proved a wise and compassionate judge and keeper of the peace. He soon became a respected leader in this new U.S. territory, highly regarded even by the conquered Mexicans. Colton's diary, published as *Three Years in California* (1850), is one of the gems of California literature. The following selections are taken from that book.

———— ◦◦ ◅◼▻ ◦◦ ————

WEDNESDAY, AUG. 5. We have in one apartment of our prison two Californians, confined for having robbed a United States courier, on his way from Monterey to San Francisco, with public dispatches. They have not yet been tried. Yesterday they applied to me

31

for permission to have their guitars. They stated that their situation was very lonely, and they wanted something to cheer it. Their request was complied with; and last evening, when the streets were still, and the soft moonlight melted through the grates of their prison, their music streamed out upon the quiet air with wonderful sweetness and power. Their voices were in rich harmony with their instruments, and their melodies had a wild and melancholy tone. They were singing, for aught they knew, their own requiem.

MONDAY, AUG 10. The fecundity of the Californians is remarkable, and must be attributed in no small degree to the effects of the climate. It is no uncommon sight to find from fourteen to eighteen children at the same table, with their mother at their head. There is a lady of some note in Monterey, who is the mother of twenty-two living children. The youngest is at the breast, and must soon, it is said, relinquish his place to a new-comer, who will, in all probability, be allowed only the same brevity of bliss.

FRIDAY, AUG. 14. Sixty of a tribe of wild Indians, who live in the mountains, about two hundred miles distant, made a descent a few days since upon a farm within thirty miles of Monterey, and carried off a hundred horses. Twenty of the tribe, with the chief, remained behind to secure further booty. Intelligence of this having reached Capt. Mervin, he dispatched a mounted force, apprehended them in their ambush, and brought them to Monterey, and delivered them over to our court for trial.

They were as wild a looking set of fellows as ever entered a civil tribunal. The chief was over seven feet high, with an enormous blanket wrapped round him and thrown over the shoulder like a Spanish cloak, which set forth his towering form to the best advantage. His long black hair streamed in darkness down to his waist. His features strikingly resembled those of Gen. Jackson. His forehead was high, his eye full of fire, and his mouth betrayed great decision. His step was firm; his age must have been about fifty. He entered the court with a civil but undaunted air. When asked why he permitted the men of his tribe to steal horses, he replied that the men who took the horses were not properly members of his tribe, that they had recently attached themselves to him, and now, that he had found them horse-thieves, he should cut them. I could get at no satisfactory evidence that he, or the twenty with him, had actively assisted those who took off the horses. I delivered them over to Capt. Mervin, who commanded the military occupation of the town.

The United States troops were formed into a hollow square, and they were marched into the centre where they expected to be shot, and still not a muscle shook, and the features of each were as set as if chiselled from marble. What must have been their unbetrayed surprise, when Capt. Mervin told them they were acquitted by the tribunal! He then told the chief he should recognize him as king of the tribe—that he must not permit any of his men to commit the slightest depredations on the citizens, that he should hold him responsible for the conduct of his tribe, and that he must come and report himself and the condition of his tribe every two moons. To all this the chief fully assented.

They were then taken on board the frigate, where the crew had been mustered for the occasion. Here they were told how many ships, men, and guns we had at our command; so much to inspire them with awe: and now for their good will. The whole party were rigged out with fresh blankets, and red handkerchiefs for each, which they use as a turban. The chief was attired in a uniform of one of our tallest and stoutest officers: navy buttons, epauletts, sword, cap with a gold band, boots, and spurs; and a silver chain was put about his neck, to which a medal was attached, recognizing him as the high chief of the tribe. He looked every inch a chief. The band struck up Hail Columbia, and they departed, vowing eternal allegiance to the Americans. The sailors were delighted with these savages, and half envied them their wild life.

MONDAY, AUG. 17. A complaint was lodged in my court this morning, involving the perplexities of a love-matter. The complainant is a Californian mother, who has a daughter rather remarkable for her personal attractions. She has two rival suitors, both anxious to marry her, and each, of course, extremely jealous of the attentions of the other, and anxious to outdo him in the fervency and force of his own assiduities. The family are consequently annoyed, and desire the court to interfere in some way for their repose. I issued an order that neither of the rival suitors should enter the house of the complainant, unless invited by her, till the girl had made up her mind.

TUESDAY, AUG. 18. The ado made to reach the hand of the undecided girl shows how very rare such specimens of beauty are in these parts. She has nothing to recommend her as a sober, industrious, frugal housekeeper. She knows how to dance, to play on the guitar and sing, and that is all. She would be as much lost in the kitchen as a dolphin on dry land. She would do to dress flowers in the balcony of a millionaire, but as the wife of a Californian, her children would go without a stocking, and her husband without a shirt. Her two suitors own, probably, the apparel which they have on and the gay horses which they ride, but neither of them has a *real* in his pocket. Yet they are quite ready to be married: just as if the honey-moon had a horn of plenty instead of a little urn of soft light, which gushes for a few brief nights, and then leaves its devotee like one of the foolish virgins, whose lamp had gone out!

THURSDAY, AUG. 20. An Indian was brought before me to-day, charged with having stolen a horse. He was on his way, it appears, to Monterey, and when within thirty miles, his own horse having given out, he turned him adrift, and lassoed one belonging to another man, which he rode in, and then set him at liberty as he had his own. The owner arrived soon after, recovered his horse, and had the Indian arrested, who confessed the whole affair, and only plead in excuse that his own horse had become too tired to go further. I sentenced the Indian to three months' labor on the public works. He seemed at first very much surprised at what he considered the severity of the sentence; but said he should work his time out faithfully, and give me no further trouble. As he was half-naked, I ordered him comfortable apparel, and then delivered him over to Capt. Mervin, to be employed in excavating a trench around the newly-erected fort.

THURSDAY, AUG. 27. Nothing puzzles me so much as the absence of a penitentiary system. There are no work-houses here; no buildings adapted to the purpose; no tools, and no trades. The custom has been to fine Spaniards, and whip Indians. The discrimination is unjust, and the punishments ill suited to the ends proposed. I have substituted labor; and have now eight Indians, three Californians, and one Englishman at work making adobes. They have all been sentenced for stealing horses or bullocks. I have given them their task: each is to make fifty adobes a day, and for all over this they are paid. They make seventy-five, and for the additional twenty-five each gets as many cents. This is paid to them every Saturday night, and they are allowed to get with it any thing but rum. They are comfortably lodged and fed by the government. I have appointed one of their number captain. They work in the field; require no other guard; not one of them has attempted to run away.

SUNDAY, AUG. 30. The wild Indians here have a vague belief in the soul's immortality. They say, "as the moon dieth and cometh to life again, so man, though he die, will again live." But their future state is material; the wicked are to be bitten by serpents, scorched by lightning, and plunged down cataracts; while the good are to hunt their game with bows that never lose their vigor, with arrows that never miss their aim, and in forests where the crystal streams roll over golden sands. Immortal youth is to be the portion of each; and age, and pain, and death, are to be known no more.

SATURDAY, SEPT. 5. I encountered on my hunting excursion to-day a wild Indian, with a squaw and papoose. They were on horses, he carrying his bow, with a large quiver of arrows hung at his side, and she with a child in the bunt of her blanket, at the back. They were dashing ahead in the wake of their dogs, which were in hot chase of a deer. The squaw stuck to her fleet animal as firmly as the saddle in which she sat, and took but little heed of the bogs and gullies over which she bounded. His glance was directed to a ridge of rocks, over which he seemed to expect the deer to fly from the field of wild oats through which the chase lay. I watched them till they disappeared in their whirlwind speed over the ridge. Whether the deer fell into their hands or escaped, I know not; but certainly I would not hazard my neck as they did theirs for all the game even in the California forests. But this, to them, is life; they seek no repose between the cradle and the grave.

TUESDAY, SEPT. 8. We have had for the last five days hardly an hour of sunshine, owing to the dense fogs which prevail here at this season. These murky vapors fill the whole atmosphere; you seem to walk in them alone, like one threading a mighty forest. A transcendentalist might easily conceive himself a ghost, wandering among the cypresses of a dead world. But, being no ghost or transcendentalist, I had a fire kindled, and found refuge from the fog in its cheerful light and warmth.

SATURDAY, SEPT. 19. I encountered to-day a company of Californians on horseback, bound to a picnic, each with his lady love on the saddle before him. He, as in duty bound, rides behind, throws his feet forward into the stirrups, his left hand holds the reins, his right encircles and sustains her, and there she rides safe as a robin in its nest; sprigs of evergreen, with wild flowers, wave in her little hat, and larger clusters in his; both are gayly attired, and smiles of light and love kindle in their dark expressive eyes. Away they gallop over hill and valley, waking the wild echoes of the wood. One of my hunting dogs glanced at them for a while, and seemed so tickled, he had to plunge into the bushes to get rid of his mirth.

MONDAY, SEPT. 21. A Californian mother came to me to-day to plead her son out of prison. He had driven off a herd of cattle which had another owner, and sold them, and I had sentenced him to the public works for a year. She felt as a good mother must feel for her son, and plead for his liberation with a pathos that half shook my resolution. Nothing but an iron sense of duty kept me firm. There is something in a mother's tears which is almost irresistible; she wept and trembled, and would have kneeled, but I would not let her. I lifted her to her feet, and told her I once had a mother, and knew what her sorrows were. I told her I would liberate her son if I could, but it was impossible; law and justice were against it. But if he behaved well, I would take off a few months from the close of the year; and in the mean time she might see him as often as she desired. She thanked me, lingered as if she would plead again, and departed. What depths there are in a mother's soul!

WEDNESDAY, SEPT. 23. I was waked this morning by sounds of merriment in the street. Day had only begun to glimmer, and its beam was contending with the glare of rockets, flashing over the lingering shadows of night. The child which I had visited a few evenings since had died, and this was its attendant ceremony to the grave. It had become, in the apprehension of those who formed the procession, a little angel—and they were expressing their joy over the transformation. The disruption of ties which bound it here—its untimely blight—and the darkness of the grave—were all forgotten. Its little coffin was draped in white, and garlanded with flowers; and voices of gladness, ringing out from childhood and youth, heralded its flight to a better world.

THURSDAY, SEPT. 24. An Englishman called at the court to-day, and desired me to issue a warrant for the apprehension of his mistress, who he said had run away and carried off a rich shawl and diamond breastpin which did not belong to her. I told him, when he entered into a criminal compact of that kind with a person, he might expect just such results as he had experienced,—and as for a warrant, I should issue none, and would not if she had carried off every thing in his house, and him too; for I should consider the community quit of two persons who could in no way benefit its morals. He looked not a little surprised at this decision, shrugged his shoulders, and departed. The first thing a foreigner does here is to provide himself with a horse; the second, with a mistress; the third, with a pack of cards. These, with a bottle of aguardiente, are his capital for this world and the next. This is true of many, but not all; there are some high and honorable exceptions.

SATURDAY, SEPT. 26. The Indians here are practical Thomsonians or Hydropathists; they sweat for every kind of disease. Their bath is a large ground-oven, to which you descend by a flight of narrow steps, and which has a small aperture at the top for the escape of the smoke. In the centre of this they build a fire, close the entrance, and shut themselves in till the temperature reaches an elevation which throws them into a profuse perspiration. They then rush out and plunge themselves into a stream of cold water. This is repeated every day till the disease leaves or death comes.

But many, without any ailment, resort to this bath as a luxury. They will stay in the oven till they are hardly able to crawl out and reach the stream. It is great fun for the more sturdy ones to lift out the exhausted and dash them in the flood. You hardly expect to see them rise again, but up they come, and regain the earth full of life and vigor. The reaction is instantaneous, and the effect, I have no doubt, in many cases beneficial. It, at least, gives them a good washing, which they would hardly get without, and which they too often need. The Indian also takes to the water to quench the flames of rum. His poor mortal tenement is often wrapped in such a conflagration. It would be a good thing if all the rum-drinkers could be marched once a week under the falls of Niagara.

MONDAY, SEPT. 28. When Monterey was taken by our squadron, an order was issued by the commander-in-chief that all the grog-shops should be closed. The object of this was to prevent disorder among the populace and among the sailors, whose duties as a patrol confined them to the shore. It was with great difficulty that this order could be enforced. All moderate fines failed to secure its observance. The price of aguardiente rose to four and five dollars the bottle, more than ten times its original cost: for such a premium the shopkeeper would run the hazard of the penalty.

We searched for it as for hid treasures, but only in one instance found its hiding-place. This was in a chimney, hanging about midway from the top. When discovered, the shopkeeper laughed as loudly as they who made the search. He was fined, not for having grog in his chimney, for that is a very good place for it, but for retailing it at his counter. An offer of four or five dollars from a customer never failed to bring down a bottle.

SATURDAY, OCT. 3. A heavy mist hung over the landscape this morning till the sun was high in the heavens, and many began to predict rain, a phenomenon which I have not yet witnessed in California. But towards noon the mist departed like a shadow dissolved in light. The scorched hills lifted their naked summits, and the deep ravines revealed their irregular lines of lingering verdure. In these the cattle still graze, though the streams which once poured their waters through them exist now only in little motionless pools, hardly sufficient to drift a duck. A stranger looking at these hills might be excused if he inquired the distance to Sodom. It would never enter his most vagrant dreams that he had reached that land towards which the tide of emigration was rolling over the cliffs of the Rocky Mountains.

FRIDAY, OCT. 9. The trouble of young and old here is the flea. The native who is thoroughly inured to his habits may little heed him, but he keeps the stranger in a constant nettle. One would suppose, from his indiscriminate and unmitigated hostility, he considered himself the proprietor of all California. Indeed, he does seem to be the genuine owner of the soil, instead of a tenant at will. It is true he may construct no dwellings, but he will plant himself in every nook and corner of the one which you may construct. He jumps into your cradle, jumps with you all along through life, and well would it be for those who remain if he jumped with you out of it. But no, he remains still; and grief for your loss will half forget its bereavement in parrying his assaults.

SUNDAY, OCT. 11. Another bright and beautiful Sabbath has dawned; but there is little here to remind one of its sacredness. A few of the larger stores are closed, but the smaller shops are all open. More liquors are retailed on this day than any other three. I have the power to close these shops, and shall do it.

SATURDAY, NOV. 7. In Monterey, as in all other towns that I have ever seen, crimes are perpetrated mostly at night. The Indian, however, steals when the temptation presents itself, and trusts luck for the consequences. And in truth if any being has a right to steal, it is the civilized Indian of California. All the mission lands, with their delicious orchards, waving grain, flocks and herds, were once his, and were stolen from him by the white man. He has only one mode of retaliating these wrongs.

THE DEVIL IN MONTEREY

Grace MacFarland

Spanish California abounded in legends and super-
stitions, most of which today are lost or forgotten. The
following tales are supposed to have been told to
Mrs. MacFarland in 1915 by Carmel Mission's "first
custodian and prince of storytellers"—an old man
then living in retirement in Monterey. They were originally published in two *Overland Monthly* install-
ments (November and December, 1915) under the
title "Myths of Monterey."

An Avenue of Crosses

When Commodore Sloat captured Monterey, Mission San Carlos was, in the language of an American
officer who visited it at that time, "A quaint old church,
falling to decay, with crumbling tower and belfry, broken roofs, and long lines of mud built dwellings, all in
ruins." Its doorways were choked with sand, its paths
hidden by weeds, for there were no worshipers at San
Carlos.

All who journeyed from Monterey southward along
the coast must travel the old Mission road, which
came to be called the Avenue of Crosses.

Almost every tree and stump beside the road bore its rude cross made of twigs or tules, or whatever other material the traveler had found handy.

The Evil One held high carnival among the ancient cypresses and moss hung pines on the road to Carmelo, and only by erecting crosses could they escape his baleful influence and skilfully hidden snares.

Even with all these precautions, many weird adventures befell the wayfarer who was so unfortunate as to be compelled to travel the forest road after dark.

Satan's Chickens

An old lady, Senora Migueles, living on a ranch below Carmelo, once came to Monterey to do some shopping. She stayed in town rather late, and just as she was starting on the Mission road, homeward bound, a heavy fog blew in, making it dark as night.

At the Avenue of Crosses she stopped her noisy cart, got out, fastened a twig cross to the nearest tree, climbed back into the cart and drove on, all the while devoutly telling her beads.

When she rounded the turn at the hill top which shut Monterey from view, Signora Migueles heard the soft "cluck-cluck" of a mother hen and the frightened "peep-peep" of a lost chick. She recalled stories of traps set by Satan for unwary ones, and listened long and earnestly. There was no mistaking that noise.

No harm could befall her, she felt sure, because of the cross and her carefully numbered beads. One more hen and a brood of chicks would help greatly on the ranch. She got out and began peering among the bushes. No sign of either hen or chick.

She finally decided to abandon the search, and much perturbed, clambered back into her cart. As she grasped the reins ready to start off, the long sought hen flew into a nearby tree.

Senora Migueles said the hen had a forked tale and one foot was a cloven hoof.

The Cloven Hoof

A cloven hoof where some other sort of foot should have been was very frequently the only way in which travelers recognized the manifestations of Satan.

Young Senor Galverez was galloping along the Mission road on his way to a fandango at the Washington Hotel in Monterey, singing and thinking of Marie, the pretty maid whom he was courting. So busy was he with these thoughts that he forgot to fasten a cross on the Avenue of Crosses.

In the midst of the forest, he was startled by a baby crying. It was such a pitiful cry that he pulled his horse up short, listening intently. The crying continued.

Some more of the Indians' doings, he thought. They must have stolen the baby, then become frightened and left it there.

He searched among the weeds and bushes and soon found the baby. With it in his arms, Senor Galvarez mounted his horse and galloped on.

As he cuddled the baby closer to keep it warm, he crossed himself. Immediately one tiny foot peeped out from the long dress. It was a cloven hoof.

Realizing that this was a snare of the Devil, and no human baby, he hurled it against the nearest tree. The babe, with an awful shriek, vanished into thin air.

Senor Galvarez continued his journey without further molestation, but henceforth did not neglect to put a cross on some tree along the Avenue of Crosses.

A Dare

A group of young profligates were scoffing one evening at the tales of adventure on Carmel road. The boldest suddenly startled them all by saying that he had just as soon walk that road alone at midnight.

The others picked up his idle words and proposed to put him to the test that very night. He agreed. As proof that he actually went to San Carlos, he was to drive a specially marked nail into the Mission wall.

Shortly before midnight he wrapped his Spanish cloak about him, took hammer and marked nail, and set out, singing a love song as he went.

Every rod of the way grew longer than the last; at each step the blackness seemed heavier; his feet dragged; the night was full of noises; his song died away in a frightened cry.

At last he saw, close ahead, the dim form of the Mission, staggered up to it, raised his hand and drove the nail into the wall. Terrified by the sound of his own hammer he turned to run away. He could not move; something held him fast as though bound with iron to the wall.

Next morning his friends, coming to see the outcome of their "dare," found him still standing by the wall, dead. The nail was driven through one corner of his cloak, holding him there, even in death.

Such vengeance was wreaked on those who desecrated the Queen of California's Mission.

Mission Meadows

Dire punishment frequently fell on the heads of those who desecrated even the Mission grounds where the neophytes and Padres slept.

When the Americans took possession of California the Missions had already been deprived of most of their land by Royal Decree. There was no one to fix the boundaries or defend the rights of these fast crumbling buildings. The Franciscans had been driven out. The pressing need of establishing and maintaining a government left the American officials no time for attending to land claims.

In the fertile valley of El Rio Carmelo many Gringo ranchers settled. One of these, being very greedy for land, carefully plowed the fields to the very walls of San Carlos. The thrifty farmer did not pause in his furrows when his plow turned up skulls and skeletons. Land was worth almost a dollar an acre, and he wanted a big crop.

Buzzards came to wail over the bones, long stripped of any flesh, which his plowing laid bare. Indians refused to work there. Crows and ravens feasted on the broadly scattered seed. Harvest time found the field as barren as spring had left it.

The farmer's wife died before another planting season. Two sons who sowed the second spring went insane in the midst of their work and killed each other. A daughter ran away with a man who only abused her, and before harvest time she, too, was dead. The Mission Meadows bore no crop.

Then the farmer ceased to plow and plant on the

graves, and reaped no more punishment for his wanton desecration of the tombs of San Carlos.

Silver

Bancroft, the historian, recounts a mining legend of the Monterey hills that has persisted until the present day.

While California was still a Mexican province, many Americans settled and established trading companies at Monterey and other ports. It was easy for the Mexicans to dispose of many things to these Gringoes about which they might have had to answer embarrassing questions had the government officials been consulted.

Senora Marie Romero, a widow who had gone to some hot springs back in the hills to cure her rheumatism, was one who took advantage of this opportunity.

With the aid of her two children she mined a little silver near her house, smelted it and sold the crudely shaped bars to Captain Cooper, a Gringo trader.

Some of the Mexican officials, learning from the Captain the source of his silver bars, determined to find the mine and take it as contraband mining. They found Marie Romero in bed with her rheumatism and unable to get up at all. The children denied all knowledge of the mine. Though the officers searched every nook of the nearby hills, they could never find it nor catch them at their mining.

Yet, somewhere in the hills just back of Monterey near the hot spring is Marie Romero's silver mine with an undug fortune for its finder.

BLOODY SUNDAYS

Richard L. Sandwick

Cock fights, bull fights, and bull and bear contests were popular, well-attended amusements in Spanish-speaking California, much to the horror of many Americans. After the American conquest most such sport was officially prohibited, though many such events continued to be held. From the *Overland Monthly* (March, 1903) comes this account of early Monterey's sporting life.

————◆◄◆►◆————

It is hard for the stranger to realize as he looks on the old tile-covered adobes of Monterey, small, many of them scarcely more than huts, that these houses once sheltered the proud owners of nearly all the valuable land from Sacramento to Santa Barbara. Yet such was the case. Families who held large ranchos as far off as Santa Clara or San Luis Obispo had also their city houses in the old capital.

These were the good old times before the Gringos came. Life was easy, money plenty, and amusement was the serious end of existence. It has been my good fortune to know some of those that lived this life, and to get from their lips the story of the fun that then went round.

The number of holidays and feast days was surprisingly large. Every Sunday was a fiesta, and the birthdays and weddings that intervened added still more to the merry-making.

At the end of the street by the plaza, Governor Castro had a stone corral. At the entrance to this, on each side of the gate, a mounted vaquero had taken his stand. The bull was driven out of the enclosure. When he had run a short distance from the riders a signal was given and they galloped down the street after him. The one that reached the animal first, seized his tail, turned it around the pommel of his saddle, and guiding his horse a little to the side, threw the bull completely off his feet. Quick as a flash the vaquero leaped from his horse, and with a short rope tied the bull's legs together and left him helpless on the ground. So skillful were the vaqueros at this that the contest was usually won by him who had the best mount, and could reach the bull first.

Then there was a cock race. A rooster was buried in the sand, only the head above ground and that well greased. A half dozen horsemen raced to get it, bending low from the saddle, and he was judged victor who succeeded in pulling up the bird by the head, or, if it stuck too fast in the sand, in pulling the head from the body.

Spain seems to be the only country that has handed down the sports of the Roman amphitheatre. The bull fights are no doubt survivals of the gladiatorial shows that once delighted the populace of Rome. There were bull-fights in Monterey in the olden times such as are known in Spain and Mexico. But more frequent, as affording greater amusement, was the bull-and-bear fight. A grizzly was lassoed by two or more vaqueros and dragged to the scene of combat, and the monarch of the herd was brought to give him battle. I talked with an old lady who saw one of these fights from the rear porch of the old Pacific House in 1847.

The beasts were within the stone corral, still partly standing, and were fastened together by a long chain. They thus interfered with one another enough to provoke a fight. The leading citizens and their families occupied the porch of the adobe hotel; the rabble lined the fence-tops.

The bull began the fight by charging the grizzly with his horns. A blow from the grizzly's paw did not stop the onset. In a moment they were rolling over each other in the dust. But the bear finally, though badly gored, got his teeth fastened into the bull's neck, and the bull was pulled to his knees. His tongue hung out. This was what the bear wanted. He got his claw into the mouth, pulling the tongue out still further, and then bit it off. With this the bull gave up the contest, and soon after both animals were dispatched.

The people in Monterey still remember Augustin Escobar, the hunter, who encountered and slew a bear with his knife in the woods where Pacific Grove now stands. It is said that this man was afterward induced to fight a bear for the delectation of the people at a fiesta in Monterey. With only a knife as a weapon, he rolled his serape or heavy cloak about his left arm and shoulder as a shield from the terrible claws. The crowd got the worth of their money; for not only was the bear killed, but Escobar carried to the end of his days, two ugly claw marks down face and chest that made him interesting, if hideous. These sights must have been degrading and it is a source of pride to know that our government put a stop to all such shows in the early fifties.

THE OLD PACIFIC CAPITAL

Robert Louis Stevenson

Exhausted, impoverished, and gravely ill with tuberculosis, twenty-nine-year-old Robert Louis Stevenson arrived in Monterey in 1879. He had come halfway around the world to find and woo Fanny Osbourne, a California woman seven years his senior, married with three children, but with whom he had fallen hopelessly in love two years before in France. The young author did find Fanny and did eventually marry her. Theirs is one of California's—one of the world's—great love stories. Stevenson spent three months in Monterey—waiting for Fanny to start divorce proceedings. While he waited he explored the region afoot, hiking into the mountains and pine forests, walking the lonely beaches and headlands. His descriptions of the peninsula are filled with a sense of discovery—the ocean with its "haunting presence"; the woods where he found it "difficult to turn homeward"; the fogs, "vast, wet, melancholy"; the old society of Monterey, about to "perish, like a lower race, before the millionaire vulgarians of the Big Bonanza." During his stay Stevenson made many friends, among them the genial, generous Frenchman, Jules Simoneau, in whose restaurant he dined almost daily. Simoneau's customers even took up a collection to underwrite Stevenson's two-dollar-a-week salary as a reporter for the local paper—without Stevenson knowing it. Today Simoneau's Plaza (site of the restaurant) and the nearby Steven-

53

son House, where the author lived and wrote, are Monterey landmarks. The following excerpts are taken from the Bigelow and Scott edition of *The Works of Robert Louis Stevenson,* 1906.

The Woods and The Pacific

The Bay of Monterey has been compared by no less a person than General Sherman to a bent fishing-hook; and the comparison, if less important than the march through Georgia, still shows the eye of a soldier for topography. Santa Cruz sits exposed at the shank; the mouth of the Salinas river is at the middle of the bend; and Monterey itself is cosily ensconced beside the barb. Thus the ancient capital of California faces across the bay, while the Pacific Ocean, though hidden by low hills and forest, bombards her left flank and rear with never-dying surf. In front of the town, the long line of sea-beach trends north and northwest, and then westward to enclose the bay. The waves which lap so quietly about the jetties of Monterey grow louder and larger in the distance; you can see the breakers leaping high and white by day; at night the outline of the shore is traced in transparent silver by the moonlight and the flying foam; and from all round, even in quiet weather, the low, distant, thrilling roar of the Pacific hangs over the coast and the adjacent country like smoke above a battle.

These long beaches are enticing to the idle man. It would be hard to find a walk more solitary and at the same time more exciting to the mind. Crowds of ducks and seagulls hover over the sea. Sandpipers trot in and out by troops after the retiring waves, thrilling together in a chorus of infinitesimal song. Strange sea-tangles, new to the European eye, the bones of whales, or sometimes a whole whale's carcase, white with carrion-gulls and poisoning the wind, lie scattered here and there along the sands. The waves come in slowly, vast and green, curve their translucent necks, and burst with a surprising uproar, that runs, waxing and waning, up and down the long keyboard of the beach. The foam of these great ruins mounts in an instant to the ridge of the sand glacis, swiftly fleets back again, and is met and buried by the next breaker. The interest is perpetually fresh. On no other coast that I know shall you enjoy, in calm, sunny weather, such a spectacle of Ocean's greatness, such beauty of changing colour, or such degrees of thunder in the sound. The very air is more than usually salt by this Homeric deep.

In shore, a tract of sand-hills borders on the beach. Here and there a lagoon, more or less brackish, attracts the birds and hunters. A rough, spotty undergrowth partially conceals the sand. The crouching, hardy, live-oaks flourish singly or in thickets—the kind of wood for murderers to crawl among—and here and there the skirts of the forest extend downward from the hills, with a floor of turf and long aisles of pine-trees hung with Spaniard's Beard. Through this quaint desert the railway cars drew near to Monterey from the junction at Salinas City—though that and so many other things are now for ever altered—and it was from here that you had your first view of the old township lying in the sands, its white windmills bickering in the chill, perpetual wind, and the first fogs of the evening drawing drearily around it from the sea.

The one common note of all this country is the haunting presence of the ocean. A great faint sound of breakers follows you high up into the inland canyons; the roar of water dwells in the clean, empty rooms of Monterey as in a shell upon the chimney; go where you will, you have but to pause and listen to hear the voice of the Pacific. You pass out of the town to the southwest, and mount the hill among the pine woods. Glade, thicket, and grove surround you. You follow winding sandy tracks that lead nowhither. You see a deer; a multitude of quail arises. But the sound of the sea still follows you as you advance, like that of wind among the trees, only harsher and stranger to the ear; and when at length you gain the summit, out breaks on every hand and with freshened vigour that same unending, distant, whispering rumble of the ocean; for now you are on the top of Monterey peninsula, and the noise no longer only mounts to you from behind along the beach towards Santa Cruz, but from your right also, round by Chinatown and Pinos lighthouse, and from down before you to the mouth of the Carmello river. The whole woodland is begirt with thundering surges. The silence that immediately surrounds you where you stand is not so much broken as it is haunted by this distant circling rumour. It sets your senses upon edge; you strain your attention; you are clearly and unusually conscious of small sounds near at hand; you walk listening like an Indian hunter; and that voice of the Pacific is a sort of disquieting company to you in your walk.

When once I was in these woods I found it difficult to turn homeward. All woods lure a rambler onward; but in those of Monterey it was the surf that particularly invited me to prolong my walks. I would push straight for the shore where I thought it to be nearest. Indeed, there was scarce a direction that would not, sooner or later, have brought me forth on the Pacific. The emptiness of the woods gave me a sense of freedom and discovery in these excursions. I never, in all my visits, met but one man. He was a Mexican, very dark of hue, but smiling and fat, and he carried an axe, though his true business at that moment was to seek

for straying cattle. I asked him what o'clock it was, but
he seemed neither to know nor care; and when he in
his turn asked me for news of his cattle, I showed myself equally indifferent. We stood and smiled upon each
other for a few seconds, and then turned without a
word and took our several ways across the forest.

One day—I shall never forget it—I had taken a
trail that was new to me. After a while the woods began to open, the sea to sound nearer hand. I came upon
a road, and, to my surprise, a stile. A step or two further, and, without leaving the woods, I found myself
among trim houses. I walked through street after street,
parallel and at right angles, paved with sward and
dotted with trees, but still undeniable streets, and each
with its name posted at the corner, as in a real town.
Facing down the main thoroughfare—"Central Avenue," as it was ticketed—I saw an open-air temple,
with benches and sounding-board, as though for an or-
chestra. The houses were all tightly shuttered; there was
no smoke, no sound but of the waves, no moving thing.
I have never been in any place that seemed so dream-
like. Pompeii is all in a bustle with visitors, and its
antiquity and strangeness deceive the imagination; but
this town had plainly not been built above a year or
two, and perhaps had been deserted over night. Indeed,
it was not so much like a deserted town as like a scene
upon the stage by daylight and with no one on the
boards. The barking of a dog led me at last to the only
house still occupied, where a Scotch pastor and his
wife pass the winter alone in this empty theatre. The
place was "The Pacific Camp Grounds, the Christian
Seaside Resort." Thither, in the warm season, crowds
come to enjoy a life of teetotalism, religion, and flirta-
tion, which I am willing to think blameless and agreeable. The neighbourhood at least is well selected. The
Pacific booms in front. Westward is Point Pinos, with

the lighthouse in a wilderness of sand, where you will
find the lightkeeper playing the piano, making models
and bows and arrows, studying dawn and sunrise in
amateur oil-painting, and with a dozen other elegant
pursuits and interests to surprise his brave, old country
rivals. To the east, and still nearer, you will come upon
a space of open down, a hamlet, a haven among rocks,
a world of surge and screaming sea-gulls. Such scenes
are very similar in different climates; they appear homely to the eyes of all; to me this was like a dozen spots
in Scotland. And yet the boats that ride in the haven
are of a strange outlandish design; and if you walk into
the hamlet you will behold costumes and faces and
hear a tongue that are unfamiliar to the memory. The
joss-stick burns, the opium-pipe is smoked, the floors
are strewn with slips of coloured paper—prayers, you
would say, that had somehow missed their destination
—and a man, guiding his upright pencil from right to
left across the sheet, writes home the news of Monterey
to the Celestial Empire.

The woods and the Pacific rule between them the
climate of this seaboard region. On the streets of Monterey, when the air does not smell salt from the one,
it will be blowing perfumed from the resinous tree-tops
of the other. For days together a hot dry air will over-
hang the town, close as from an oven, yet healthful
and aromatic in the nostrils. The cause is not far to
seek, for the woods are afire, and the hot wind is
blowing from the hills. These fires are one of the great
dangers of California. I have seen from Monterey as
many as three at the same time, by day a cloud of
smoke, by night a red coal of conflagration in the distance. A little thing will start them, and if the wind be
favourable they gallop over miles of country faster than
a horse. The inhabitants must turn out and work like
demons, for it is not only the pleasant groves that are

destroyed; the climate and the soil are equally at stake, and these fires prevent the rains of the next winter, and dry up perennial fountains. California has been a land of promise in its time, like Palestine; but if the woods continue so swiftly to perish, it may become, like Palestine, a land of desolation.

To visit the woods while they are languidly burning, is a strange piece of experience. The fire passes through the underbrush at a run. Every here and there a tree flares up instantaneously from root to summit, scattering tufts of flame; and is quenched, it seems, as quickly. But this last is only in semblance. For after this first squib-like conflagration of the dry moss and twigs, there remains behind a deep-rooted and consuming fire in the very entrails of the tree. The resin of the pitch pine is principally condensed at the base of the bole and in the spreading roots. Thus, after the light, showy, skirmishing flames, which are only as the match to the explosion, have already scampered down the wind into the distance, the true harm is but beginning for this giant of the woods. You may approach the tree from one side, and see it, scorched indeed from top to bottom, but apparently survivor of the peril. Make the circuit, and there, on the other side of the column, is a clear mass of living coal, spreading like an ulcer; while underground, to their most extended fibre, the roots are being eaten out by fire, and the smoke is rising through the fissures to the surface. A little while, and, with a nod of warning, the huge pine-tree snaps off short across the ground and falls prostrate with a crash. Meanwhile the fire continues its silent business; the roots are reduced to a fine ash; and long afterwards, if you pass by, you will find the earth pierced with radiating galleries, and preserving the design of all these subterranean spurs, as though it were the mould for a new tree instead of the print of an old one. These pitch pines of

Monterey are, with the single exception of the Monterey cypress, the most fantastic of forest trees. No words can give an idea of the contortion of their growth; they might figure without change in a circle of the nether hell as Dante pictured it; and at the rate at which trees grow, and at which forest fires spring up and gallop through the hills of California, we may look forward to a time when there will not be one of them left standing in that land of their nativity. At least they have not so much to fear from the axe, but perish by what may be called a natural, although a violent death; while it is man in his short-sighted greed that robs the country of the nobler redwood. Yet a little while and perhaps all the hills of seaboard California may be as bald as Tamalpais.

I have an interest of my own in these forest fires, for I came so near to lynching on one occasion, that a braver man might have retained a thrill from the experience. I wished to be certain whether it was the moss, that quaint funereal ornament of California forests, which blazed up so rapidly when the flame first touched the tree. I suppose I must have been under the influence of Satan; for instead of plucking off a piece for my experiment, what should I do but walk up to a great pine tree in a portion of the wood which had escaped so much as scorching, strike a match, and apply the flame gingerly to one of the tassels. The tree went off simply like a rocket; in three seconds it was a roaring pillar of fire. Close by I could near the shouts of those who were at work combating the original conflagration. I could see the waggon that had brought them tied to a live oak in a piece of open; I could even catch the flash of an axe as it swung up through the underwood into the sunlight. Had anyone observed the result of my experiment my neck was literally not worth

a pinch of snuff; after a few minutes of passionate ex-
postulation I should have been run up to a convenient
bough.

"To die for faction is a common evil;
But to be hanged for nonsense is the devil."

I have run repeatedly, but never as I ran that day.
At night I went out of town, and there was my own
particular fire, quite distinct from the other, and burning as I thought with even greater spirit.

But it is the Pacific that exercises the most direct
and obvious power upon the climate. At sunset, for
months together, vast, wet, melancholy fogs arise and
come shoreward from the ocean. From the hill top
above Monterey the scene is often noble, although it
is always sad. The upper air is still bright with sunlight;
a glow still rests upon the Gabelano [Gabilan] Peak;
but the fogs are in possession of the lower levels; they
crawl in scarves among the sand-hills; they float, a little
higher, in clouds of a gigantic size and often of a wild
configuration; to the south, where they have struck the
seaward shoulder of the mountains of Santa Lucia, they
double back and spire up skyward like smoke. Where
their shadow touches, colour dies out of the world. The
air grows chill and deadly as they advance. The trade-
wind freshens, the trees begin to sigh, and all the windmills in Monterey are whirling and creaking and filling
their cisterns with the brackish water of the sands. It
takes but a little while till the invasion is complete.
The sea, in its lighter order, has submerged the earth.
Monterey is curtained in for the night in thick, wet,
salt, and frigid clouds; so to remain till day returns;
and before the sun's rays they slowly disperse and re-
treat in broken squadrons to the bosom of the sea. And

yet often when the fog is thickest and most chill, a few steps out of the town and up the slope, the night will be dry and warm and full of inland perfume.

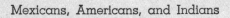

Mexicans, Americans, and Indians

The history of Monterey has yet to be written. Founded by Catholic missionaries, a place of wise beneficence to Indians, a place of arms, a Mexican capital continually wrested by one faction from another, an American capital when the first House of Representatives held its deliberations, and then falling lower and lower from the capital of the State to the capital of a county, and from that again, by the loss of its charter and town lands, to a mere bankrupt village, its rise and decline is typical of that of all Mexican institutions and even Mexican families in California. Nothing is stranger in that strange State than the rapidity with which the soil has changed hands. The Mexicans, you may say, are all poor and landless, like their former capital; and yet both it and they hold themselves apart and preserve their ancient customs and something of their ancient air.

The town, when I was there, was a place of two or three streets, economically paved with sea sand, and two or three lanes, which were watercourses in the rainy season, and were, at all times, rent up by fissures four or five feet deep. There were no street lights. Short sections of wooden sidewalk only added to the dangers of the night, for they were often high above the level of the roadway, and no one could tell where they would be likely to begin or end. The houses were, for the most part, built of unbaked adobe brick, many of them old for so new a country, some of very elegant proportions, with low, spacious, shapely rooms, and walls so thick that the heat of summer never dried them to the heart. At the approach of the rainy season a deathly chill and a graveyard smell began to hang about the lower floors; and diseases of the chest are common and fatal among housekeeping people of either sex.

There was no activity but in and around the saloons, where people sat almost all day long playing cards. The smallest excursion was made on horseback. You would scarcely ever see the main street without a horse or two tied to posts, and making a fine figure with their Mexican housings. It struck me oddly to come across some of the "Cornhill" illustrations of Mr. Blackmore's "Erema," and see all the characters astride on English saddles. As a matter of fact, an English saddle is a rarity even in San Francisco, and, you may say, a thing unknown in all the rest of California. In a place so exclusively Mexican as Monterey, you saw not only Mexican saddles but true vaquero riding— men always at the hand-gallop up hill and down dale, and round the sharpest corner, urging their horses with cries and gesticulations and cruel rotatory spurs, checking them dead with a touch, or wheeling them right-about-face in a square yard. The type of face and character of bearing is surprisingly un-American. The first ranged from something like the pure Spanish, to something, in its sad fixity, not unlike the pure Indian, although I do not suppose there was one pure blood of either race in all the country. As for the second, it was a matter of perpetual surprise to find, in that world of absolutely mannerless Americans, a people full of deportment, solemnly courteous, and doing all things with grace and decorum. In dress they ran to colour and bright sashes. Not even the most Americanised could always resist the temptation to stick a red

rose into his hatband. Not even the most Americanised
would condescend to wear the vile dress hat of civilisa-
tion. Spanish was the language of the streets. It was
difficult to get along without a word or two of that
language for an occasion. The only communications in
which the population joined were with a view of
amusement. A weekly public ball took place with great
etiquette, in addition to the numerous fandangoes in
private houses. There was a really fair amateur brass
band. Night after night serenaders would be going about
the street, sometimes in a company and with several
instruments and voices together, sometimes severally,
each guitar before a different window. It was a strange
thing to lie awake in nineteenth century America, and
hear the guitar accompany, and one of these old, heart-
breaking Spanish love songs mount into the night air,
perhaps in a deep baritone, perhaps in that high-
pitched, pathetic, womanish alto which is so common
among Mexican men, and which strikes on the unaccustomed ear as something not entirely human but altogether sad.

The town, then, was essentially and wholly Mexican;
and yet almost all the land in the neighbourhood was
held by Americans, and it was from the same class,
numerically so small, that the principal officials were
selected. This Mexican and that Mexican would de-
scribe to you his old family estates, not one rood of
which remained to him. You would ask him how that
came about, and elicit some tangled story back-fore-
most, from which you gathered that the Americans
had been greedy like designing men, and the Mexicans
greedy like children, but no other certain fact. Their
merits and their faults contributed alike to the ruin of
the former landholders. It is true they were improvi-
dent, and easily dazzled with the sight of ready money;
but they were gentlefolk besides, and that in a way

which curiously unfitted them to combat Yankee craft. Suppose they have a paper to sign, they would think it a reflection on the other party to examine the terms with any great minuteness; nay, suppose them to observe some doubtful clause, it is ten to one they would refuse from delicacy to object to it. I know I am speaking within the mark, for I have seen such a case occur, and the Mexican, in spite of the advice of his lawyer, has signed the imperfect paper like a lamb. To have spoken in the matter, he said, above all to have let the other party guess that he had seen a lawyer, would have "been like doubting his word." The scruple sounds oddly to one of ourselves, who has been brought up to understand all business as a competition in fraud, and honesty itself to be a virtue which regards the carrying out but not the creation of agreements. This single unworldly trait will account for much of that revolution of which we are speaking. The Mexicans have the name of being great swindlers, but certainly the accusation cuts both ways. In a contest of this sort, the entire booty would scarcely have passed into the hands of the more scrupulous race.

Physically the Americans have triumphed; but it is not yet entirely seen how far they have themselves been morally conquered. This is, of course, but a part of a part of an extraordinary problem now in the course of being solved in the various States of the American Union. I am reminded of an anecdote. Some years ago, at a great sale of wine, all the odd lots were purchased by a grocer in a small way in the old town of Edinburgh. The agent had the curiosity to visit him some time after and inquire what possible use he could have for such material. He was shown, by way of answer, a huge vat where all the liquors, from humble Gladstone to imperial Tokay, were fermenting together. "And what," he asked, "do you propose to call this?"

"I'm no very sure," replied the grocer, "but I think it's going to turn out port." In the older Eastern States, I think we may say that this hotch-potch of races is going to turn out English, or thereabout. But the problem is indefinitely varied in other zones. The elements are differently mingled in the South, in what we may call the Territorial belt, and in the group of States on the Pacific coast. Above all, in these last, we may look to see some monstrous hybrid—whether good or evil, who shall forecast? but certainly original and all its own.

In my little restaurant at Monterey, we have sat down to table day after day, a Frenchman, two Portuguese, an Italian, a Mexican, and a Scotchman; we had for common visitors an American from Illinois, a nearly pure blood Indian woman, and a naturalised Chinese; and from time to time a Switzer and a German came down from country ranches for a night. No wonder that the Pacific coast is a foreign land to visitors from the Eastern States, for each race contributes something of its own. Even the despised Chinese have taught the youth of California, none indeed of their virtues, but the debasing use of opium. And chief among these influences is that of the Mexicans.

The Mexicans, although in the State, are out of it. They still preserve a sort of international independence, and keep their affairs snug and to themselves. Only four or five years ago Vasquez, the bandit, his troop being dispersed and the hunt too hot for him in other parts of California, returned to his native Monterey, and was seen publicly in her street and saloons, fearing no man. The year that I was there there occurred two reputed murders. As the Montereyans are exceptionally vile speakers of each other and of everyone behind his back, it is not possible for me to judge how much truth there may have been in these reports; but in the one case everyone believed, and in the other some suspected, that there had been foul play; and nobody dreamed for an instant of taking the authorities into their counsel. Now this is, of course, characteristic enough of the Mexicans; but it is a noteworthy feature that all the Americans in Monterey acquiesced without a word in this inaction. Even when I spoke to them upon the subject, they seemed not to understand my surprise: they had forgotten the traditions of their own race and upbringing, and become, in a word, wholly Mexicanised.

Again, the Mexicans, having no ready money to speak of, rely almost entirely in their business transactions upon each other's worthless paper. Pedro the penniless pays you with an I O U from the equally penniless Miguel. It is a sort of local currency by courtesy. Credit in these parts has passed into a superstition. I have seen a strong, violent man struggling for months to recover a debt, and getting nothing but an exchange of waste paper. The very storekeepers are averse to asking cash payments, and are more surprised than pleased when they are offered. They fear there must be something under it, and that you mean to withdraw from them your custom. I have seen the enterprising chemist and stationer begging me with fervour to let my account run on, although I had my purse open in my hand; and partly from the commonness of the case, partly from some remains of that generous old Mexican tradition which made all men welcome to their tables, a person may be notoriously both unwilling and unable to pay, and still find credit for the necessaries of life in the stores of Monterey. Now this villainous habit of living upon "tick" had grown into Californian nature. I do not only mean that the American and European storekeepers of Monterey are as lax as Mexicans; I mean that American farmers in many parts of the State expect unlimited credit, and profit by it in the meanwhile, without a thought for consequences. Jew storekeepers have already learned the advantage to be gained from this; they lead on the farmer into irretrievable indebtedness, and keep him ever after as their bond-slave, hopelessly grinding in the mill. So the whirlgig of time brings in its revenges, and except that the Jew knows better than to foreclose, you may see Americans bound in the same chains with which they themselves had formerly bound the Mexicans. It seems as if certain sorts of follies, like certain sorts of grain, were natural to the soil rather than to the race that holds and tills it for the moment.

In the meantime, however, the Americans rule in Monterey County. The new county seat, Salinas City, in the bald, corn-bearing plain under the Gabelano Peak, is a town of a purely American character. The land is held, for the most part, in those enormous tracts which are another legacy of Mexican days, and form the present chief danger and disgrace of California; and the holders are mostly of American or British birth. We have here in England no idea of the troubles and inconveniences which flow from the existence of these large landholders—land thieves, land sharks, or land grabbers, they are more commonly and plainly called. Thus the townlands of Monterey are all in the hands of a single man. How they came there is an obscure, vexatious question, and, rightly or wrongly, the man is hated with a great hatred. His life has been repeatedly in danger. Not very long ago, I was told, the stage was stopped and examined three evenings in succession by disguised horsemen thirsting for his blood. A certain house on the Salinas road, they say, he always passes in his buggy at full speed, for the squatter sent him warning long ago. But a year since he was publicly pointed out for death by no less a man

than Mr. Dennis Kearney. Kearney is a man too well
known in California, but a word of explanation is
required for English readers. Originally an Irish dray-
man, he rose, by his command of bad language, to
almost dictatorial authority in the State; throned it
there for six months or so, his mouth full of oaths,
gallowses, and conflagrations; was first snuffed out last
winter by Mr. Coleman, backed by his San Francisco
Vigilantes and three Gatling guns; completed his own
ruin by throwing in his lot with the grotesque Green-
backer party; and had at last to be rescued by his old
enemies, the police, out of the hands of his rebellious
followers. It was while he was at the top of his fortune
that Kearney visited Monterey with his battle-cry against
Chinese labour, the railroad monopolists, and the land
thieves; and his one articulate counsel to the Montereyans was to "Hang David Jacks." Had the town been
American, in my private opinion this would have been
done years ago. Land is a subject on which there is
no jesting in the West, and I have seen my friend
the lawyer drive out of Monterey to adjust a competition of titles with the face of a captain going into
battle and his Smith-and-Wesson convenient to his
hand.

On the ranch of another of these landholders you
may find our old friend, the truck system, in full op-
eration. Men live there, year in year out, to cut timber
for a nominal wage, which is all consumed in supplies.
The longer they remain in this desirable service the
deeper they will fall in debt—a burlesque injustice in
a new country, where labour should be precious, and
one of those typical instances which explains the pre-
vailing discontent and the success of the demagogue
Kearney.

In a comparison between what was and what is in
California, the praisers of times past will fix upon the

Indians of Carmello. The day of the Jesuit has gone
by, the day of the Yankee has succeeded, and there is
no one left to care for the converted savage. The mission church is roofless and ruinous; sea breezes and
sea fogs, and the alternation of the rain and sunshine,
daily widening the breaches and casting the crockets
from the wall. As an antiquity in this new land, a
quaint specimen of missionary architecture, and a me-
morial of good deeds, it had a triple claim to preserva-
tion from all thinking people; but neglect and abuse
have been its portion. There is no sign of American
interference, save where a headboard has been torn
from a grave to be a mark for pistol bullets. So it is
with the Indians for whom it was erected. Their lands,
I was told, are being yearly encroached upon by the
neighbouring American proprietor, and with that exception no man troubles his head of the Indians of
Carmel. Only one day in the year, the day before
our Guy Faux, the *padre* drives over the hill from
Monterey; the little sacristy, which is the only covered portion of the church, is filled with seats and dec-
orated for the service; the Indians troop together, their
bright dresses contrasting with their dark and melancholy faces; and there, among a crowd of somewhat
unsympathetic holiday makers, you may hear God
served with perhaps more touching circumstances than
in any other temple under heaven. An Indian, stone
blind and about eighty years of age, conducts the singing; other Indians compose the choir; yet they have
the Gregorian music at their finger ends, and pronounce
the Latin so correctly that I could follow the meaning as they sang. The pronunciation was odd and
nasal, the singing hurried and staccato. "In saecula
saeculo-ho-horum," they went, with a vigorous aspirate
to every additional syllable. I have never seen faces
more vividly lit up with joy than the faces of these

Indian singers. It was to them not only the worship of God, nor an act by which they recalled and commemorated better days, but was besides an exercise of culture, where all they knew of art and letters was united and expressed. And it made a man's heart sorry for the good fathers of yore, who had taught them to dig and to reap, to read and to sing, who had given them European mass-books which they still preserve and study in their cottages, and who had now passed away from all authority and influence in that land—to be succeeded by greedy land thieves and sacrilegious pistol-shots. So ugly a thing our Anglo-Saxon Protestantism may appear beside the doings of the Society of Jesus.

But revolution in this world succeeds to revolution. All that I say in this paper is in a paulo-past tense. The Monterey of last year exists no longer. A huge hotel [the Del Monte] has sprung up in the desert by the railway. Three sets of diners sit down successively to table. Invaluable toilettes figure along the beach and between the live oaks; and Monterey is advertised in the newspapers, and posted in the waiting-rooms at railway stations, as a resort for wealth and fashion. Alas for the little town! it is not strong enough to resist the influence of the flaunting caravanserai, and the poor, quaint, penniless native gentlemen of Monterey must perish, like a lower race, before the millionaire vulgarians of the Big Bonanza.

CHINATOWN

Mary H. Field

During the 1870s, a small shanty community of Chinese fishermen and their families appeared along the shorefront between Monterey and the Christian Seaside Resort at Pacific Grove. This exotic little colony existed quietly here for about thirty years, its most prominent, and apparently most annoying, feature being the occasional odors that came from the fish and squid hung out to dry in the sun. Around the turn of the century resentments toward the Chinese began to surface. The Chinatown property was becoming valuable and several attempts were made to evict the inhabitants and develop the area. Then, on the night of May 16, 1906, fire broke out at the west end of Chinatown. According to Monterey historian Augusta Fink, "Many felt sure arson was its cause. Strong headwinds fanned the blaze and the Pacific Grove volunteer fire department, for some reason, had difficulty obtaining sufficient water. . . . No one knows how many Chinese were killed. They seemed to vanish, while their possessions were pillaged by looters from neighboring towns. . . . The Chinese community of humble, happy, hardworking people was gone, virtually overnight." Mary H. Field, the author of the following sketch (which appeared in the *Overland Monthly*, December, 1887), was a California author of some renown and a cultural leader in the Pacific Grove community in the 1880s.

A little farther on is the huddle of wretched shanties where the Chinese colony of fisher-folk live in such squalor as beggars description. . . . They were celebrating their New Year and keeping "open house." The procession [of visitors] filed along the cliff path one breezy morning, and all were soon stumbling among the long racks for drying fish which are the outlying defenses of this "Chinatown."

Here were two little girls at play, though one was loaded down with a fat baby, done up in a queer little patchwork contrivance and strapped to her back. Each had a little tin wagon, which she dragged along, and the one with the encumbrance seemed almost as agile and care free as the other. . . .

They found everywhere men crowded in the dingy little rooms gambling with Chinese dice. Women were occasionally visible at the small windows, and children were abundant on the streets. They were barefooted and dirty, but like the grown folks, dressed in new dark blue suits, and evidently having a jolly time with playthings and sweetmeats of their own peculiar fashion. Over every door was a strip of red cloth caught up with tinsel paper, the Mongolian's regular festive decoration. Doors stood open, and in two or three of the little six by nine apartments, families were seated around a table, eating uncanny dishes or drinking tea out of tiny cups. The presence of visitors excited no attention and called out no civilities. Often on a shelf on one side there was a little shrine of tinsel paper and red cloth, before which little joss sticks were stuck, and a lamp or taper was burning. No idol was visible, but a strip of red paper with black characters painted upon it seemed to represent either an ancestor or a god, nearly identical things in Chinese theology. Sometimes a box was set before this shrine heaped with votive offerings of rice, tea, and fish. Dirt and confusion reigned everywhere from the greasy black tables and floors out to the uncleanly street, yet everybody looked fat and healthy. In the centre of the crooked, narrow street was a heap of stones crowned with a larger shrine for worship. Joss sticks were stuck in every crevice, and absurd attempts at decoration, in the way of rags and flowers, were visible. The ground was strewn far and near with exploded fire-crackers. Evidently there had been a wild orgy the night before with unlimited fire-works.

In one little hovel a young and pretty Chinese woman was sitting on a table, sewing on a child's apron, while three little children were playing around her. She could understand and talk a little in English, and politely returned her callers' "Happy New Year." Her name was Ah Ying, she said, and she pointed out her husband, a gray-haired Chinaman painting his boat down on the beach.

A lovely Christian woman has opened a Mission School near this forlorn colony and is working faithfully for their uplifting. This suggested a theme for conversation.

"Do your children go to Miss N—'s school, Mrs. Ying?" asked Filiola.

"Yes. She belly good woman," said Ah Ying, brightening perceptibly. One could see that a grateful heart was here.

In summer these people do a large business in catching and drying fish. Their boats can be seen far out on the bay from morning till night; and sometimes all night long their red lanterns gleam across the water, and their shrill voices are heard in counsel or command as they ply their great trident-like spears among shoals of fish. But in winter most of their business stops, especially the drying of fish, and consequently Chinatown is far less malodorous in winter. The fastidious summer visitor at Monterey gives them a wide berth, and the path along the cliffs from the grove to the town is almost deserted. It is hard for the delicately housed and fed to feel or recognize a human tie with these poor pagan aliens.

Carmel Mission, 1909.

(All photos courtesy of the Bancroft Library, University of California.)

Mary Austin's
"wick-i-up," 1912.

Ocean Avenue, Carmel, 1909.

Robinson Jeffers.

George Sterling posing on rock.

Del Monte horse-drawn carry all.

Del Monte Hotel, 1912.

Notley's Landing.

HOTBED OF SOULFUL CULTURE, VORTEX OF EROTIC ERUDITION. CARMEL IN CALIFORNIA, WHERE AUTHOR AND ARTIST FOLK ARE ESTABLISHING THE MOST AMAZING COLONY ON EARTH.

Willard Huntington Wright

In early 1910 a witty and sophisticated young reporter from southern California turned up in Carmel, spent a week visiting with the artists and writers, asking questions and making notes for a newspaper article to appear in the Los Angeles *Times*. The young man's name was Willard Huntington Wright and his article, which appeared in May of that year, must have created a bit of a stir in the Carmel bohemian community. Wright poked fun at all of the major and minor Carmelites—their dress, their hair, their speech, their eccentricities, and the results of their labors in behalf of Art. His caricatures of certain prominent individuals, Mary Austin and Upton Sinclair, for example, are devastatingly sarcastic. Wright later went on to New York, became editor of *Smart Set*, published books and wrote for many eastern magazines. His fame today rests primarily

on his Philo Vance mystery stories ,written under the
pseudonym S. S. Van Dine.

Carmel-By-The-Sea is a very temperamental town.
Situated five miles from Monterey in a huge pine
grove which slopes to the sea, Carmel has been blessed
with much natural beauty. Its abundant foliage, lush
ravines, picturesque hills and its austere, implacable
coast have caught the imagination of the artist-folk. The
result is that Carmel has a great deal of temperament
that orginally was not indigenous. At present it is a
hotbed of soulful culture, a vortex of animated erudi-
tion. The artistic bacilli are so numerous that in-
noculation is imminent even to the visiting pachyderm.

Of late it has become the magnetizing center for
writers, near writers, notsonear writers, distant writers,
poets, poetines, artists, daubers, sloydists, and those
aspiring ladies who spend their days smearing up with
paint what would otherwise be very serviceable pieces
of canvas. In addition, there are at least twenty college professors, a club of well-meaning neophytes of
the arts-and-crafts, esoteric Yogi, New Thoughters, Em-
manuel Movers—and last (but not the least, O Lord),
the dramatists.

Conversationally, Carmel is polysyllabic. Scenery,
the soul, and art have infinite possibilities for discussion
and are indulged in almost exclusively. When I arrived at Carmel, it was a dead-heat on these subjects,
although immediately after my coming art got in the
lead, with the scenery a close second. For two days
the soul spurted, and the scenery and art dropped far
behind. But when I left, the scenery had it her own
way. In summer, however, art is the only entry. It is
discussed from sun to sun. It is the only intellectual
pabulum during the dog-days. At the end of August

the topic of art has been worn to a frazzle. It takes it
the remainder of the year to recuperate.

Nor is the vocabulary employed in the conversation-
al clinic that of the humdrum man. No, indeed: Bi-
zarre and rococo words flourish. Were I not afraid of
appearing erudite, I would say that a sententious ses-
quipedalianism characterized the Carmelian repartee.
To be in the verbal swim in Carmel one must have
handy cataclysmic variations for the commonest phrases.
For instance, if I were going to say "the leaves are
green," I would fly at it in some such manner as
this: "Yon arboreal appendages are emerald-hued."

I sneaked in upon the town unawares. I assumed an
expression of supreme intellectual agony. Near me
walked two figures. I tentatively approached and stood
ethereally by. This is what I heard:

"The fingers of my soul clutch too intensely the visible manifestations of reality. I lose all."

"Ay, tragedy is tragic, but emotionalism is bitter-
sweet. Now my mind is prehensile. No recess of living
evades me. The harmony of being—"

I staggered on.

In a shady pine shadow sat a masculine tuft of hair
in front of an easel. He was doing the sunset. But the
sunset was divinely indifferent—it didn't know what
was happening to it. From a bosky glade near by, an
athletic figure snarked forth. It was Jack London, the
progenitor of the red corpuscle in literature. He was
joined by two languorous females, and they in turn
gathered about them other persons of various dimensions and temperaments. And toward the beach they
plodded merrily, calling to the houses as they passed:
"Come, the sunset!"

When the beach was reached, they seated themselves along a lupined hummock of posies, and what
they did to that sunset was a-plenty. It was an adjectival

orgy. One fair young thing, gazing rapturously intoned the following:

"Tis like a wassalious Bacchante, reeling her westering rout."

"Tis as a Cyclopean blacksmith," corrected Mary Austin, remembering her Browning, "striking frenzied sparks from the anvil of the horizon."

"Isn't it sweet?" (Was it Lucia Chamberlain's voice?)

Here London entered the commentative ring. "Sweet? Hell! That sunset has guts!"

The conversation then ascended into words of five syllables and over. So I retreated to the Pine Inn and inquired for Alice MacGowan. Translating the directions into every-day English by use of a pocket dictionary, with which I had armed myself before my invasion, I wandered off down the beach toward the large and imposing house situated on a hill overlooking the Carmel bay.

When Miss MacGowan appeared she informed me that I had broken into an inspiration. The vision of a jail loomed before me. Breaking into an inspiration at Carmel was probably a penal offense, like breaking into a house in an ordinary community. And it was a clear case against me. I was red-handed. So I apologized humbly, fearing I might be placed under arrest. But nothing tragic happened. The lady proved very charming and kind. Through her I met the Carmelites.

At this point allow me to paint a cursory picture of the town. There is in Carmel but one street that looks worthy of the name. The other byways are rustic and unpaved. It is considered a crime to cut the trees or shrubbery, and the result is that the many little bungalows of which the town is comprised, are hidden from sight until one is very near to them. Carmel has the general appearance of being a primeval, uninhabited spot, and little does one suspect what mighty and cul-

tured things are going on there. There is a Roycrofty
hotel on the main street, one or two grocery stores, a
bakery, a plumbing establishment, a candy shop, a
livery stable, and a drug store—oh, let us not forget the
drug store. I put emphasis on this establishment, for
what would seem a very irrelevant reason, namely, that
Carmel is a temperance town. Parenthetically, I would
suggest to the stranger within Carmel's gates that he
get an introduction to the druggist. He is a man worth
knowing.

A few of the lots in Carmel townsite were sold under
an old regime and are not amenable to the temperance
law now in vogue. With a county license, the owners of
these lots could erect parlors of conviviality and intro-
duce the Demon Rum to the public. The promoters of
Carmel have their fears of what may happen any day.
The deeds to these lots hang over their heads—a sort of
bottle of Damocles. Any day the red wine may flow in
Carmel. But at present the drys have it.

One reaches Carmel by stage from Monterey, over
the Carmel hill. Nothing so vulgar as a railroad has
dared penetrate into this sanctum sanctorum of art.

There are two factions in the artistic population of
Carmel. One is the Respectable Element, and the other
the Eminently Respectable element. At the head of the
one is George Sterling. The favorite beverages of this
faction are mint punch, Scotch highballs and Riesling.
Its favorite pastimes, when it is not engaged in artistic
pursuits are singing and imbibing the aforementioned
beverages. Jack London, James Hopper, Fred Bechdolt, Fra Lafler, Herbert Herron, Lucia Chamberlain,
Xavier Martinez and Upton Sinclair are on the Receiv-
ing Committee of this faction, although recently Sinclair has shunted to the Eminently Respectables, because of the chemical reaction of spiritous fluids on the
peritoneal coating of the stomach.

The Eminently Respectables are led by the two charming sisters, Alice MacGowan and Grace Mac-Gowan Cooke. Arthur H. Vachell, artist, brother of the novelist [Horace A. Vachell], is the male chaperon and most dependable member of this faction. Arnold Genthe holds forth here and also Mary Austin. The habits of this faction are impeccable. Bedtime at 10 o'clock, and nothing more inhibitional than milk in the way of liquid febrifuges. To this faction a cigarette is the symbol of the devil; and unconventionalities are the Old Boy's insidious artifices. The sunsets and the old homely virtues for them. No sporty vocal ensembles in tonsorial harmonics concerning "O you kid," and kindred subjects, could tempt them from the virtuous serenity of their ways.

The attitude of the outsiders—that is, of the uninspired and the inartistic—toward the intellectually elite and the esthetically cultured, has in it mingled pride and disgust. The ones without the pale don't exactly know what to make of these rarefied souls, but at the same time they feel that in some subtle and recondite way these souls add to the dignity and superiority of the place.

When I first inquired of the stage driver at Monterey as to the artistic condition of Carmel, a look of pride accompanied the information that there were "a heap of real swell writers and artists in Carmel." Later, as we were driving over the hill in a stage, which had had a long and strenuous past, behind a horse that long ago had forgotten its youth, a sudden steep pull necessitated a halt. The poor beast struggled but could not move. The fat driver arose and began a furious stream of epithets. Having exhausted all the derogatory and infuriate side of his vocabulary, he settled back in disgust and looked painfully at the horse. He was ransacking his brain for some final anathema. For the moment the lexicon of mortality seemed inadequate to express his true emotions toward the beast. But suddenly he arose and gripped his gad. There was a note of satisfaction in his voice:

"Giddap, you damn artist!" he said. The damn artist proceeded.

———— ▸◂——◆——▸◂ ————

Carmel is the home of art in all of its branches and in all of its stages of development. Its products during the year consist chiefly of novels, near-novels, pseudo-novels, quasi-novels, dramas, poems, fustians, essays, rhapsodies, sagas, stuffed short stories, best-sellars, zymotic romances, Kammererzachlungen, pottery, burnt leather, mission chairs and fancy knitting. . . .

The plumber of Carmel has subscribed to the Harvard Classics. The butcher reads Browning, and the liveryman wears long hair. These unsuspecting people are caught, as it were, in the whirlpool of temperament into which Carmel has been drawn.

I have never seen so much temperament en masse. There is any amount of poetic (minor) temperament, dramatic temperament, artistic temperament, esthetic and esoteric temperament, religious, scientific, pedagogical and literary temperament: plain, grilled, en casserole, and Bordelaise temperament; nerves, hysteria, neurasthenia and all the other complications.

The temperament of Carmel manifests itself in many strange ways. Besides in the creation of the plastic and graphic arts, it breaks out sartorially, dietetically and hirsutically. For instance, there is a great deal of neckwear in Carmel. Men and women alike are addicted to flowing cravats. These long, trailing Windsors are a sign of genius. It is impossible to be a genius without a necktie that looks like a fat woman's sash. It is the symbol, the trade-mark. Any why not? How could we distinguish a genius from an uninspired stockbroker were it not for this sign?

The temperament of Carmel, however, has affected but a few victims dietetically. Chief among these are Upton Sinclair. . . . No one would dare attempt to unseat Sinclair from his digestive divan. He has usurped this particular pose. And he has done it with a vengeance. He has left no gastronomic stone unturned. He is the Sherlock Holmes of the pork sausage, the ultimate germ eradicator, the baccilli Pinkerton, the microbe's dilemma, the milk-can poet, the final living authority on the dangerous and deadly pastime of eating. . . .

We were at Point Lobos one day on a picnic, and when lunch time came the ladies showed their culinary ability by preparing a most wonderful luncheon of fried fish, enchiladas, abalone, mussels, shrimp salad and other delicacies. When the luncheon call sounded, Sinclair approached the table with an air of dietetic superiority, and running a scornful eye over the steaming dishes, exclaimed, haughtily:

"Gormandize on poison if you will. As for me, I prefer my health." And seating himself on a dank rock by the beach, he took a raw tomato from his pocket and consumed it with masticatory unction.

But probably the chief temperamental asset of Carmel is hair. There is a great deal of hair in this chosen city of the elect. You meet it wherever you go. I venture the assertion that Carmel has more hair per capita than any town in America—unless it is East Aurora. And there are all different kinds of hair, from the raven locks of Mary Austin to the pale saffron down of Burgdorff: from the straight rigidity of Martinez's mop to the fancy ringlets of Mr. Heron. There are hardly two collections of hair just alike. They have but one characteristic in common, and that is length. All the hair one meets in Carmel is long. The Carmelite's contention is, "Art is long: why not hair?"

P.S.—There is a barber in Carmel, but I hear he has an independent income.

The Carmelites include a great many well-known writers and artists who hope to be well known.

It is here that Jack London creates his red-blooded yarns. Between chapters, he skirts the fiords in search of the abalone. His menu consists solely of underdone duck and Martini cocktails.

Alice MacGowan and Grace MacGowan-Cooke, consanguinary and literary sisters, hold forth at Carmel, and write best sellers. They are the most indefatigable workers in the place. . . .

In Carmel lives the wassail bard. George Sterling. But Sterling is not a real poet; his sense of humor is too keen, and he is too interested in life. In the early morning he may be heard at his wood-pile, heaving valiantly away at pitch-pine logs. And a little later, one may behold him hoeing in his garden. Like Yeats at Innisfree, Sterling has nine bean rows. He raises potatoes, and catches his own fish. He lives the life of the outdoor Indian. He is happily married, unlike many of the Carmelites, and, when he writes, it is for his own amusement. I do not wish to imply that Sterling has no temperament, for he has. But he keeps it well under cover.

Mary Austin, however, is a radiating center of temperament. Temperament exudes from her and stands out around her like an aural integument. It seethes and bubbles from her like vertiginous heat-waves. Her principal occupation is wandering among the pines with her hair flowing, and discussing the microcosmic aspect of neoplatonic theurgy. There have been many aspirants for Mary Austin's place as the temperamental mad mollah, but she does not ride side-saddle on her hobby, and any unhorsing process would be extremely difficult. She builds wickiups in which to write, and never uses them. She has dramatized her temperament so that it is almost a perfect piece of art.

Henry Anderson Lafler, the shag-pated troglodyte, is a Carmelite. So is Lucia Chamberlain, the Blessed Damozel of the mystery tale. She wanders by the sea plucking posies and blowing Egyptian diety rings into the empyrean.

It is at Carmel that Upton Sinclair holds forth and shakes the foundations of our social universe with feverish novels.

From San Francisco comes Xavier Martinez, the painter, whose features can only be seen at close range. There is evidently some bitter feud between Martinez and the immortal profession. His head resembles a huge black chrysanthemum. Only by parting the hirsute curtain in front can he look out upon the world.

To Carmel came Arnold Genthe, San Francisco's society photographer, the esthete of the camera, the ne plus ultra of the off-focus portrait. Genthe can photograph you so that you will have no idea that it is you. He has mastered the device of blending his sitters into the background so that no one can tell where the figure leaves off and the background begins. But a sad fate overtook Genthe at Carmel. Between his cottage and the sea an anesthetic merchant built a two-story abode. And now there floats in Genthe's vision, not the daffodil, but a washing on the line. By Jove's covenant, imagine it! Laundered shirts! Sacr' artiste! Genthe fled back to San Francisco, his esthetic nature irremediably impaired. Ah, me—or rather, Ah, him! The elect have tragedies of which we—the uninspired—know naught!

Then, at Carmel, there are Fred Bechdolt, writer of

short stories, Michael Williams (Upton Sinclair's right-hand dietetician) and Ina Coolbrith, the poet.

Chris Jorgensen has a large house at Carmel. Jorgensen is a rapid-fire society artist. After a hasty breakfast, he paints a canvas and sells it to a tourist at noon. After a hurried repast he paints another large canvas and sells it at dinner time. He was the instigator of the installation of electric lights in Carmel Valley. His object was to paint another picture after dinner and sell it at midnight. I asked someone why he kept cows, and they said it was to have always at hand a fresh supply of butter to paint with. (This, of course, isn't true.) . . .

Herbert Herron is the esthete of Carmel. He is an unappreciated poet who writes long iambic pentameter affairs concerning Actaeon and kindred personages. His original name was Herbert Herron Peet, but some poetine remarked that "Peet" sounded like the noise that a hen makes so Mr. Peet dropped the unpoetic cognomen. Under Mr. Herron's house is a massive vault of reinforced concrete with triple plate doors of iron, and combination springs and padlocks. In this is kept his poetry. And nor time nor cyclone nor fire nor editor nor critic can ever reach his epic wares. They are being carefully preserved for posterity, and Mr. Herron sees to it that no masterpiece from his pen shall be lost. Posthumous his fame may be, but the concrete vault will at least protect his manuscript from commercial editors and the wrath of the elements.

But I cannot tabulate any more. Life is short, and the list of Carmelian artists is long. There they flourish, and talk their strange talk, and paint their weird pictures and write their anaemic poetry, and fabricate their undramatic dramas, and turn out their novels which rust for the want of editorial appreciation.

But who would scoff at the quotidian fry of artists?

Surely not I. I have no desire to see them either hanged or exiled. A writer or a poet or a painter or a creator of crafty things, no matter how atrocious the finished product may be, seems a trifle better than the man who spends his life accumulating money. In them is the embryonic instinct toward what is beautiful rather than what is commercial. . . . May their tribe increase. May they fill the world with worthless strophes. May they niggle with paints to the end of their days. For seven thousand years let them sit in the pine groves of Carmel and mix their colors and their metaphors.

BILLY AND SAXON

Jack London

Jack London was never a resident-member of the
Carmel bohemia. He was, nevertheless, a close friend
of George Sterling and made at least two trips to
Carmel, one in 1905 and another in 1910. These brief
visits resulted in a hauntingly beautiful piece of
Monterey Peninsula writing—a story which became
a part of his novel *Valley of the Moon* (1913). The
novel tells of a young man and wife struggling to
escape the entrapments of industrial society by starting a new life on the land. Billy, an uneducated Oakland teamster and former prizefighter, and his musi-
cal young wife, Saxon, discover Carmel almost by
accident during a journey down the coast in search
of homestead acreage. Saxon's first impression of
Carmel has probably been the response of thousands
of awe-struck travelers to the Peninsula. The character of Mark Hall in the story is a thinly disguised
George Sterling (creator of the famous "Abalone
Song"), and the other writers and artists are almost
certainly patterned after the real-life Carmel "crowd"
London knew.

They had taken the direct county road across the
hills from Monterey, instead of the Seventeen Mile
Drive around by the coast, so that Carmel Bay came

upon them without any fore-glimmerings of its beauty. Dropping down through the pungent pines, they passed woods-embowered cottages, quaint and rustic, of artists and writers, and went on across wind-blown rolling sandhills held to place by sturdy lupins and nodding with pale California poppies. Saxon screamed in sudden wonder of delight, then caught her breath and gazed at the amazing peacock-blue of a breaker, shot through with golden sunlight, overfalling in a mile-long sweep and thundering into white ruin of foam on a crescent beach of sand scarcely less white.

How long they stood and watched the stately procession of breakers, rising from out the deep and wind-capped sea to froth and thunder at their feet, Saxon did not know. She was recalled to herself when Billy, laughing, tried to remove the telescope basket from her shoulders.

"You kind of look as though you was goin' to stop a while," he said. "So we might as well get comfortable."

"I never dreamed it, I never dreamed it," she repeated, with passionately clasped hands. "I . . . I thought the surf at the Cliff House was wonderful, but it gave no idea of this. ——Oh! Look! LOOK! Did you ever see such an unspeakable color? And the sunlight flashing right through it! Oh! Oh! Oh!"

At last she was able to take her eyes from the surf and gaze at the sea-horizon of deepest peacock-blue and piled with cloud-masses, at the curve of the beach south to the jagged point of rocks, and at the rugged blue mountains seen across soft low hills, landward, up Carmel Valley.

"Might as well sit down an' take it easy," Billy indulged her. "This is too good to want to run away from all at once."

Saxon assented, but began immediately to unlace her shoes.

"You ain't a-goin' to?" Billy asked in surprised delight, then began unlacing his own.

But before they were ready to run barefooted on the perilous fringe of cream-wet sand where land and ocean met, a new and wonderful thing attracted their attention. Down from the dark pines and across the sandhills ran a man, naked save for narrow trunks. He was smooth and rosy-skinned, cherubic-faced, with a thatch of curly yellow hair, but his body was hugely thewed as a Hercules'.

"Gee!—must be Sandow," Billy muttered low to Saxon.

But she was thinking of the engraving in her mother's scrapbook and of the Vikings on the wet sands of England.

The runner passed them a dozen feet away, crossed the wet sand, never pausing, till the froth wash was to his knees while above him, ten feet at least, upreared a wall of overtopping water. Huge and powerful as his body had seemed, it was now white and fragile in the face of that imminent, great-handed buffet of the sea. Saxon gasped with anxiety, and she stole a look at Billy to note that he was tense with watching.

But the stranger sprang to meet the blow, and, just when it seemed he must be crushed, he dived into the face of the breaker and disappeared. The mighty mass of water fell in thunder on the beach, but beyond appeared a yellow head, one arm out-reaching, and a portion of a shoulder. Only a few strokes was he able to make ere he was compelled to dive through another breaker. This was the battle—to win seaward against the sweep of the shoreward-hastening sea. Each time he dived and was lost to view Saxon caught her breath and clenched her hands. Sometimes, after the passage of a breaker, they could not find him, and when they did he would be scores of feet away, flung there like a chip by a smoke-bearded breaker. Often it seemed he must fail and be thrown upon the beach, but at the end of half an hour he was beyond the outer edge of the surf and swimming strong, no longer diving, but topping the waves. Soon he was so far away that only at intervals could they find the speck of him. That, too, vanished, and Saxon and Billy looked at each other, she with amazement at the swimmer's valor, Billy with blue eyes flashing.

"Some swimmer, that boy, some swimmer," he praised. "Nothing chicken-hearted about him.——Say, I only know tank-swimmin', an' bay-swimmin', but now I'm goin' to learn ocean-swimmin'. If I could do that I'd be so proud you couldn't come within forty feet of me. Why, Saxon, honest to God, I'd sooner do what he done than own a thousan' farms. Oh, I can swim, too, I'm tellin' you, like a fish—I swum, one Sunday, from the Narrow Gauge Pier to Sessions' Basin, an' that's miles—but I never seen anything like that guy in the swimmin' line. An' I'm not goin' to leave this beach until he comes back. ——All by his lonely out there in a mountain sea, think of it! He's got his nerve all right, all right."

Saxon and Billy ran barefooted up and down the beach, pursuing each other with brandished snakes of seaweed and playing like children for an hour. It was not until they were putting on their shoes that they sighted the yellow head bearing shoreward. Billy was at the edge of the surf to meet him, emerging, not white-skinned as he had entered, but red from the pounding he had received at the hands of the sea.

"You're a wonder, and I just got to hand it to you," Billy greeted him in outspoken admiration.

"It *was* a big surf to-day," the young man replied, with a nod of acknowledgment.

"It don't happen that you are a fighter I never heard

of?" Billy queried, striving to get some inkling of the identity of the physical prodigy.

The other laughed and shook his head, and Billy could not guess that he was an ex-captain of a Varsity Eleven, and incidentally the father of a family and the author of many books. He looked Billy over with an eye trained in measuring freshmen aspirants for the gridiron.

"You're some body of a man," he appreciated. "You'd strip with the best of them. Am I right in guessing that you know your way about in the ring?"

Billy nodded. "My name's Roberts."

The swimmer scowled with a futile effort at recollection.

"Bill—Bill Roberts," Billy supplemented.

"Oh, ho!—Not *Big* Bill Roberts? Why, I saw you fight, before the earthquake, in the Mechanic's Pavillion. It was a preliminary to Eddie Hanlon and some other fellow. You're a two-handed fighter, I remember that, with an awful wallop, but slow. Yes, I remember, you were slow that night, but you got your man." He put out a wet hand. "My name's Hazard—Jim Hazard."

"An' if you're the football coach that was, a couple of years ago, I've read about you in the papers. Am I right?"

They shook hands heartily, and Saxon was introduced. She felt very small beside the two young giants, and very proud, withal, that she belonged to the race that gave them birth. She could only listen to them talk.

"I'd like to put on the gloves with you every day for half an hour," Hazard said. "You could teach me a lot. Are you going to stay around here?"

"No. We're goin' on down the coast, lookin' for land. Just the same, I could teach you a few, and there's one thing you could teach me—surf swimmin'."

"I'll swap lessons with you any time," Hazard offered.

He turned to Saxon. "Why don't you stop in Carmel for a while? It isn't so bad."

"It's beautiful," she acknowledged, with a grateful smile, "but——" She turned and pointed to their packs on the edge of the lupins. "We're on the tramp, and lookin' for government land."

"If you're looking down past the Sur for it, it will keep," he laughed. "Well, I've got to run along and get some clothes on. If you come back this way, look me up. Anybody will tell you where I live. So long."

And, as he had first arrived, he departed, crossing the sandhills on the run.

Billy followed him with admiring eyes.

"Some boy, some boy," he murmured. "Why, Saxon, he's famous. If I've seen his face in the papers once, I've seen it a thousand times. An' he ain't a bit stuck on himself. Just man to man. Say! ——I'm beginnin' to have faith in the old stock again."

They turned their backs on the beach and in the tiny main street bought meat, vegetables, and half a dozen eggs. Billy had to drag Saxon away from the window of a fascinating shop where were iridescent pearls of abalone, set and unset.

"Abalones grow here, all along the coast," Billy assured her; "an' I'll get you all you want. Low tide's the time."

"My father had a set of cuff-buttons made of abalone shell," she said. "They were set in pure, soft gold. I haven't thought about them for years, and I wonder who has them now."

They turned south. Everywhere from among the pines peeped the quaint pretty houses of the artist folk, and they were not prepared, where the road dipped to Carmel River, for the building that met their eyes.

"I know what it is," Saxon almost whispered. "It's

an old Spanish Mission. It's the Carmel Mission, of course. That's the way the Spaniards came up from Mexico, building missions as they came and converting the Indians——"

"Until we chased them out, Spaniards an' Indians, whole kit an' caboodle," Billy observed with calm satisfaction.

"Just the same, it's wonderful," Saxon mused, gazing at the big, half-ruined adobe structure. "There is the Mission Dolores, in San Francisco, but it's smaller than this and not as old."

Hidden from the sea by low hillocks, forsaken by human being and human habitation, the church of sun-baked clay and straw and chalk-rock stood hushed and breathless in the midst of the adobe ruins which once had housed its worshiping thousands. The spirit of the place descended upon Saxon and Billy, and they walked softly, speaking in whispers, almost afraid to go in through the open portal. There was neither priest nor worshiper, yet they found all the evidences of use, by a congregation which Billy judged must be small from the number of the benches. Later they climbed the earthquake-cracked belfry, noting the hand-hewn timbers; and in the gallery, discovering the pure quality of their voices, Saxon, trembling at her own temerity, softly sang the opening bars of "Jesus Lover of My Soul." Delighted with the result, she leaned over the railing, gradually increasing her voice to its full strength as she sang:

"Jesus, Lover of my soul
    Let me to Thy bosom fly,
While the nearer waters roll,
    While the tempest still is nigh.
Hide me, O my Saviour, hide,

Till the storm of life is past;
Safe into the haven guide
And receive my soul at last."

Billy leaned against the ancient wall and loved her
with his eyes, and, when she had finished, he murmured,
almost in a whisper:

"That was beautiful—just beautiful. An' you ought
to a-seen your face when you sang. It was as beautiful
as your voice. Ain't it funny? ——I never think of religion except when I think of you."

They camped in the willow bottom, cooked dinner,
and spent the afternoon on the point of low rocks north
of the mouth of the river. They had not intended to
spend the afternoon, but found themselves too fascinated
to turn away from the breakers bursting upon the rocks
and from the many kinds of colorful sea life—starfish,
crabs, mussels, sea anemones, and, once, in a rock-
pool, a small devilfish that chilled their blood when it
cast the hooded net of its body around the small crabs
they tossed to it. As the tide grew lower, they gathered
a mess of mussels—huge fellows, five and six inches
long and bearded like patriarchs. Then, while Billy
wandered in a vain search for abalones, Saxon lay and
dabbled in the crystal-clear water of a rock-pool, dip-
ping up handfuls of glistening jewels—ground bits of
shell and pebble of flashing rose and blue and green
and violet. Billy came back and lay beside her, lazying
in the sea-cool sunshine, and together they watched
the sun sink into the horizon where the ocean was
deepest peacock-blue.

She reached out her hand to Billy's and sighed with
sheer repletion of content. It seemed she had never
lived such a wonderful day. It was as if all old dreams
were coming true. Such beauty of the world she had

never guessed in her fondest imagining. Billy pressed
her hand tenderly.

"What was you thinkin' of?" he asked, as they arose
finally to go.

"Oh, I don't know, Billy. Perhaps that it was better, one day like this, than ten thousand years in Oakland."

They left Carmel River and Carmel Valley behind,
and with a rising sun went south across the hills between the mountains and the sea. The road was badly
washed and gullied and showed little sign of travel.

"It peters out altogether farther down," Billy said.
"From there on it's only horse trails. But I don't see
much signs of timber, an' this soil's none so good. It's
only used for pasture—no farmin' to speak of."

The hills were bare and grassy. Only the canyons
were wooded, while the higher and more distant hills
were furry with chaparral. Once they saw a coyote slide
into the brush, and once Billy wished for a gun when
a large wildcat stared at them malignantly and declined
to run until routed by a clod of earth that burst about
its ears like shrapnel.

Several miles along Saxon complained of thirst.
Where the road dipped nearly at sea level to cross a
small gulch Billy looked for water. The bed of the
gulch was damp with hill-drip, and he left her to rest
while he sought a spring.

"Say," he hailed a few minutes afterward. "Come
on down. You just gotta see this. It'll 'most take your
breath away."

Saxon followed the faint path that led steeply down
through the thicket. Midway along, where a barbed

wire fence was strung high across the mouth of the gulch and weighted down with big rocks, she caught her first glimpse of the tiny beach. Only from the sea could one guess its existence, so completely was it tucked away on three precipitous sides by the land, and screened by the thicket. Furthermore, the beach was the head of a narrow rock cove, a quarter of a mile long, up which pent way the sea roared and was subdued at the last to a gentle pulse of surf. Beyond the mouth many detached rocks, meeting the full force of the breakers, spouted foam and spray high in the air. The knees of these rocks, seen between the surges, were black with mussels. On their tops sprawled huge sea-lions tawny-wet and roaring in the sun, while overhead, uttering shrill cries, darted and wheeled a multitude of sea birds.

The last of the descent, from the barbed wire fence, was a sliding fall of a dozen feet, and Saxon arrived on the soft dry sand in a sitting posture.

"Oh, I tell you it's just great," Billy bubbled. "Look at it for a camping spot. In among the trees there is the prettiest spring you ever saw. An' look at all the good firewood, an' . . ." He gazed about and seaward with eyes that saw what no rush of words could compass. ". . . An', an' everything. We could live here. Look at the mussels out there. An' I bet you we could catch fish. What d'ye say we stop a few days? ——It's vacation anyway—an' I could go back to Carmel for hooks an' lines."

Saxon, keenly appraising his glowing face, realized that he was indeed being won from the city.

"An' there ain't no wind here," he was recommending. "Not a breath. An' look how wild it is. Just as if we was a thousand miles from anywhere."

The wind, which had been fresh and raw across the bare hills, gained no entrance to the cove; and the beach was warm and balmy, the air sweetly pungent with the thicket odors. Here and there, in the midst of the thicket, were small oak trees and other small trees of which Saxon did not know the names. Her enthusiasm now vied with Billy's, and, hand in hand, they started to explore.

"Here's where we can play real Robinson Crusoe," Billy cried, as they crossed the hard sand from high-water mark to the edge of the water. "Come on, Robinson. Let's stop over. Of course, I'm your Man Friday, an' what you say goes."

"But what shall we do with Man Saturday!" She pointed in mock consternation to a fresh footprint in the sand. "He may be a savage cannibal, you know."

"No chance. It's not a bare foot but a tennis shoe."

"But a savage could get a tennis shoe from a drowned or eaten sailor, couldn't he?" she contended.

"But sailors don't wear tennis shoes," was Billy's prompt refutation.

"You know too much for Man Friday," she chided; "but, just the same, if you'll fetch the packs we'll make camp. Besides, it mightn't have been a sailor that was eaten. It might have been a passenger."

By the end of an hour a snug camp was completed. The blankets were spread, a supply of firewood was chopped from the seasoned driftwood, and over a fire the coffee pot had begun to sing. Saxon called to Billy, who was improvising a table from a wave-washed plank. She pointed seaward. On the far point of rocks, naked except for swimming trunks, stood a man. He was gazing toward them, and they could see his long mop of dark hair blown by the wind. As he started to climb the rocks landward Billy called Saxon's attention to the fact that the stranger wore tennis shoes. In a few minutes he dropped down from the rock to the beach and walked up to them.

"Gosh!" Billy whispered to Saxon. "He's lean enough, but look at his muscles. Everybody down here seems to go in for physical culture."

As the newcomer approached, Saxon glimpsed sufficient of his face to be reminded of the old pioneers and of a certain type of face seen frequently among the old soldiers. Young though he was—not more than thirty, she decided—this man had the same long and narrow face, with the high cheekbones, high and slender forehead, and nose high, lean, and almost beaked. The lips were thin and sensitive; but the eyes were different from any she had ever seen in pioneer or veteran or any man. They were so dark a gray that they seemed brown, and there were a farness and alertness of vision in them as of bright questing through profounds of space. In a misty way Saxon felt that she had seen him before.

"Hello," he greeted. "You ought to be comfortable here." He threw down a partly filled sack. "Mussels. All I could get. The tide's not low enough yet."

Mark Hall was their visitor's name, and he lived in a bungalow among the Carmel pines.

"But how did you ever find your way to Bierce's Cove?" he was curious to know. "Nobody ever dreams of it from the road."

"So that's its name?" Saxon said.

"It's the name we gave it. One of our crowd camped here one summer, and we named it after him. I'll take a cup of that coffee, if you don't mind."
——This to Saxon. "And then I'll show your husband around. We're pretty proud of this cove. Nobody ever comes here but ourselves. Come along. I'll show you around now. You'd better get your clothes off. Keep on only your shoes and pants, unless you've got a pair of trunks. . . . Say, where are you and your husband bound?"

When Saxon had told him of their attempt to get away from Oakland and of their quest for land, he sympathized with the first and shook his head over the second.

"It's beautiful down beyond the Sur," he told her. "I've been all over those redwood canyons, and the place is alive with game. The government land is there, too. But you'd be foolish to settle. It's too remote. And it isn't good farming land, except in patches in the canyons. I know a Mexican there who is wild to sell his five hundred acres for fifteen hundred dollars. Three dollars an acre! And what does that mean? That it isn't worth more. That it isn't worth so much; because he can find no takers. Land, you know, is worth what they buy and sell it for."

Billy, emerging from the thicket, only in shoes and in pants rolled to the knees, put an end to the conversation; and Saxon watched the two men, physically so dissimilar, climb the rocks and start out the south side of the cove. At first her eyes followed them lazily, but soon she grew interested and worried. Hall was leading Billy up what seemed a perpendicular wall in order to gain the backbone of the rock. Billy went slowly, displaying extreme caution; but twice she saw him slip, the weather-eaten stone crumbling away in his hand and rattling beneath him into the cove. When Hall reached the top, a hundred feet above the sea, she saw him stand upright and sway easily on the knife-edge which she knew fell away as abruptly on the other side. Billy, once on top, contented himself with crouching on hands and knees. The leader went on, upright, walking as easily as on a level floor. Billy abandoned the hands and knees position, but crouched closely and often helped himself with his hands.

The knife-edge backbone was deeply serrated, and into one of the notches both men disappeared. Saxon could not keep down her anxiety, and climbed out on the north side of the cove, which was less rugged and far less difficult to travel. Even so, the unaccustomed height, the crumbling surface, and the fierce buffets of the wind tried her nerve. Soon she was opposite the men. They had leaped a narrow chasm and were scaling another tooth. Already Billy was going more nimbly, but his leader often paused and waited for him. The way grew severer, and several times the clefts they essayed extended down to the ocean level and spouted spray from the growling breakers that burst through. At other times, standing erect, they would fall forward across deep and narrow clefts until their palms met the opposing side; then, clinging with their fingers, their bodies would be drawn across and up.

Near the end, Hall and Billy went out of sight over the south side of the backbone, and when Saxon saw them again they were rounding the extreme point of rock and coming back on the cove side. Here the way seemed barred. A wide fissure, with hopelessly vertical sides, yawned skywards from a foam-white vortex where the mad waters shot their level a dozen feet upward and dropped it as abruptly to the black depths of battered rock and writhing weed.

Clinging precariously, the men descended their side till the spray was flying about them. Here they paused. Saxon could see Hall pointing down across the fissure and imagined he was showing some curious thing to Billy. She was not prepared for what followed. The surf-level sucked and sank away, and across and down Hall jumped to a narrow foothold where the wash had roared yards deep the moment before. Without pause, as the returning sea rushed up, he was around the sharp corner and clawing upward hand and foot to escape being caught. Billy was now left alone. He could not even see Hall, much less be further advised by him, and so tensely did Saxon watch, that the pain in her finger-tips, crushed to the rock by which she held, warned her to relax. Billy waited his chance, twice made tentative preparations to leap and sank back, then leaped across and down to the momentarily exposed foothold, doubled the corner, and as he clawed up to join Hall was washed to the waist but not torn away.

Saxon did not breathe easily till they rejoined her at the fire. One glance at Billy told her that he was exceedingly disgusted with himself.

"You'll do, for a beginner," Hall cried, slapping him jovially on the bare shoulder. "That climb is a stunt of mine. Many's the brave lad that's started with me and broken down before we were half way out. I've had a dozen balk at that big jump. Only the athletes make it."

"I ain't ashamed of admittin' I was scairt," Billy growled. "You're a regular goat, an' you sure got my goat half a dozen times. But I'm mad now. It's mostly trainin', an' I'm goin' to camp right here an' train till I can challenge you to a race out an' around an' back to the beach."

"Done," said Hall, putting out his hand in ratification. "And some time, when we get together in San Francisco, I'll lead you up against Bierce—the one this cove is named after. His favorite stunt, when he isn't collecting rattlesnakes, is to wait for a forty-mile-an-hour breeze, and then get up and walk on the parapet of a skyscraper—on the lee side, mind you, so that if he blows off there's nothing to fetch him up but the street. He sprang that on me once."

"Did you do it?" Billy asked eagerly.

"I wouldn't have if I hadn't been on. I'd been practicing it secretly for a week. And I got twenty dollars out of him on the bet."

The tide was now low enough for mussel gathering and Saxon accompanied the men out the north wall. Hall had several sacks to fill. A rig was coming for him in the afternoon, he explained, to cart the mussels back to Carmel. When the sacks were full they ventured further among the rock crevices and were rewarded with three abalones, among the shells of which Saxon found one coveted blister-pearl. Hall initiated them into the mysteries of pounding and preparing the abalone meat for cooking.

By this time it seemed to Saxon that they had known him a long time. It reminded her of the old times when Bert had been with them, singing his songs or ranting about the last of the Mohicans.

"Now, listen; I'm going to teach you something," Hall commanded, a large round rock poised in his hand above the abalone meat. "You must never, never pound abalone without singing this song. Nor must you sing this song at any other time. It would be the rankest sacrilege. Abalone is the food of the gods. Its preparation is a religious function. Now listen, and follow, and remember that it is a very solemn occasion."

The stone came down with a thump on the white meat, and thereafter arose and fell in a sort of tom-tom accompaniment to the poet's song:

"Oh! some folks boast of quail on toast,
    Because they think it's tony;
But I'm content to owe my rent
    And live on abalone.

"Oh! Mission Point's a friendly joint
    Where every crab's a crony,

And true and kind you'll ever find
  The clinging abalone.

"He wanders free beside the sea
  Where'er the coast is stony;
He flaps his wings and madly sings—
  The plaintive abalone.

"Some stick to biz, some flirt with Liz
  Down on the sands of Coney;
But we, by hell, stay in Carmel,
  And whang the abalone."

He paused with his mouth open and stone upraised. There was a rattle of wheels and a voice calling from above where the sacks of mussels had been carried. He brought the stone down with a final thump and stood up.

"There's a thousand more verses like those," he said. "Sorry I hadn't time to teach you them." He held out his hand, palm downward. "And now, children, bless you, you are now members of the clan of Abalone Eaters, and I solemnly enjoin you, never, no matter what the circumstances, pound abalone meat without chanting the sacred words I have revealed unto you."

"But we can't remember the words from only one hearing," Saxon expostulated.

"That shall be attended to. Next Sunday the Tribe of Abalone Eaters will descend upon you here in Bierce's Cove, and you will be able to see the rites, the writers and writeresses, down even to the Iron Man with the basilisk eyes, vulgarly known as the King of the Sacerdotal Lizards."

"Will Jim Hazard come?" Billy called, as Hall disappeared into the thicket.

"He will certainly come. Is he not the Cave-Bear

Pot-Walloper and Gridironer, the most fearsome, and, next to me, the most exalted, of all the Abalone Eaters?"

Saxon and Billy could only look at each other till they heard the wheels rattle away.

"Well, I'll be doggoned," Billy let out. "He's some boy, that. Nothing stuck up about him. Just like Jim Hazard, comes along and makes himself at home, you're as good as he is an' he's as good as you, an' we're all friends together, just like that, right off the bat."

"He's old stock, too," Saxon said. "He told me while you were undressing. His folks came by Panama before the railroad was built, and from what he said I guess he's got plenty of money."

"He sure don't act like it."

"And isn't he full of fun!" Saxon cried.

"A regular josher. An' *him!*——a *poet!*"

"Oh, I don't know, Billy. I've heard that plenty of poets are odd."

"That's right, come to think of it. There's Joaquin Miller, lives out in the hills back of Fruitvale. He's certainly odd. It's right near his place where I proposed to you. Just the same I thought poets wore whiskers and eyeglasses, an' never tripped up foot-races at Sunday picnics, nor run around with as few clothes on as the law allows, gatherin' mussels an' climbin' like goats."

That night, under the blankets, Saxon lay awake, looking at the stars, pleasuring in the balmy thicket-scents, and listening to the dull rumble of the outer surf and the whispering ripples on the sheltered beach a few feet away. Billy stirred, and she knew he was not yet asleep.

"Glad you left Oakland, Billy?" she snuggled.

"Huh!" came his answer. "Is a clam happy?"

Every half tide Billy raced out the south wall over the dangerous course he and Hall had traveled, and each trial found him doing it in faster time.

"Wait till Sunday," he said to Saxon. "I'll give that poet a run for his money. Why, they ain't a place that bothers me now. I've got the head confidence. I run where I went on hands an' knees. I figured it out this way: Suppose you had a foot to fall on each side, an' it was soft hay. They'd be nothing to stop you. You wouldn't fall. You'd go like a streak. Then it's just the same if it's a mile down on each side. That ain't your concern. Your concern is to stay on top and go like a streak. An', d'ye know, Saxon, when I went at it that way it never bothered me at all. Wait till he comes with his crowd Sunday. I'm ready for him."

"I wonder what the crowd will be like," Saxon speculated.

"Like him, of course. Birds of a feather flock together. They won't be stuck up, any of them, you'll see."

Hall had sent out fish-lines and a swimming suit by a Mexican cowboy bound south to his ranch, and from the latter they learned much of the government land and how to get it. The week flew by; each day Saxon sighed a farewell of happiness to the sun; each morning they greeted its return with laughter of joy in that another happy day had begun. They made no plans, but fished, gathered mussels and abalones, and climbed among the rocks as the moment moved them. The abalone meat they pounded religiously to a verse of doggerel improvised by Saxon. Billy prospered. Saxon had never seen him at so keen a pitch of health. As for herself, she scarcely needed the little hand-mirror to know that never, since she was a young girl, had there been such color in her cheeks, such spontaneity of vivacity.

"It's the first time in my life I ever had real play," Billy said. "An' you an' me never played at all all the time we was married. This beats bein' any kind of a millionaire."

"No seven o'clock whistle," Saxon exulted. "I'd lie abed in the mornings on purpose, only everything is too good not to be up. And now you just play at chopping some firewood and catching a nice big perch, Man Friday, if you expect to get any dinner."

Billy got up, hatchet in hand, from where he had been lying prone, digging holes in the sand with his bare toes.

"But it ain't goin' to last," he said, with a deep sigh of regret. "The rains'll come any time now. The good weather's hangin' on something wonderful."

The Abalone Eaters, in two rigs and on a number of horses, descended in force on Bierce's Cove. There were half a score of men and almost as many women. All were young, between the ages of twenty-five and forty, and all seemed good friends. Most of them were married. They arrived in a roar of good spirits, tripping one another down the slippery trail and engulfing Saxon and Billy in a comradeship as artless and warm as the sunshine itself. Saxon was appropriated by the girls—she could not realize them women; and they made much of her, praising her camping and traveling equipment and insisting on hearing some of her tale. They were experienced campers themselves, as she quickly discovered when she saw the pots and pans and clothes-boilers for the mussels which they had brought.

In the meantime Billy and the men had undressed and scattered out after mussels and abalones. The girls lighted on Saxon's ukulélé and nothing would do but she must play and sing. Several of them had been to Honolulu, and knew the instrument, confirming Mercedes' definition of ukulélé as "jumping flea." Also, they knew Hawaiian songs she had learned from Mercedes, and soon, to her accompaniment, all were singing: "Aloha Oe," "Honolulu Tomboy," and "Sweet Lie Lehua." Saxon was genuinely shocked when some of them, even the more matronly, danced hulas on the sand.

When the men returned, burdened with sacks of shellfish, Mark Hall, as high priest, commanded the due and solemn rite of the tribe. At a wave of his hand, the many poised stones came down in unison on the white meat, and all voices were uplifted in the Hymn to the Abalone. Old verses all sang, occasionally some one sang a fresh verse alone, whereupon it was repeated in chorus. Billy betrayed Saxon by begging her in an undertone to sing the verse she had made, and her pretty voice was timidly raised in:

> "We sit around and gaily pound,
>   And bear no acrimony,
>   Because our ob—ject is a gob
>   Of sizzling abalone."

"Great!" cried the poet, who had winced at *ob—ject*. "She speaks the language of the tribe! Come on, children—now!"

And all chanted Saxon's lines. Then Jim Hazard had a new verse, and one of the girls, and the Iron Man with the basilisk eyes of greenish-gray, whom Saxon recognized from Hall's description. To her it seemed he had the face of a priest.

> "Oh! some like ham and some like lamb,
>   And some like macaroni;

But bring me in a pail of gin
And a tub of abalone.

"Oh! some drink rain and some champagne
Or brandy by the pony;
But I will try a little rye
With a dash of abalone.

"Some live on hope and some on dope,
And some on alimony;
But our tom-cat, he lives on fat
And tender abalone."

A black-haired, black-eyed man with the roguish face of a satyr, who, Saxon learned, was an artist who sold his paintings at five hundred apiece, brought on himself universal execration and acclamation by singing:

"The more we take, the more they make
In deep-sea matrimony;
Race-suicide cannot betide
The fertile abalone."

And so it went, verses new and old, verses without end, all in glorification of the succulent shellfish of Carmel. Saxon's enjoyment was keen, almost ecstatic, and she had difficulty in convincing herself of the reality of it all. It seemed like some fairy tale or book story come true. Again, it seemed more like a stage, and these the actors, she and Billy having blundered into the scene in some incomprehensible way. Much of the wit, she sensed she did not understand. Much she did understand. And she was aware that brains were playing as she had never seen brains play before. The puritan streak in her training was astonished and shocked by some of the broadness; but she refused to sit in judgment. They *seemed* good, these light-hearted young people; they certainly were not rough or gross as were many of the crowds she had been with on Sunday picnics. None of the men got drunk, although there were cocktails in vacuum bottles and red wine in a huge demijohn.

What impressed Saxon most was their excessive jollity, their childlike joy, and the childlike things they did. This effect was heightened by the fact that they were novelist and painters, poets and critics, sculptors and musicians. One man, with a refined and delicate face—a dramatic critic on a great San Francisco daily, she was told—introduced a feat which all the men tried and failed at most ludicrously. On the beach, at regular intervals, planks were placed as obstacles. Then the dramatic critic, on all fours, galloped along the sand for all the world like a horse and for all the world like a horse taking hurdles he jumped the planks to the end of the course.

Quoits had been brought along, and for a while these were pitched with zest. Then jumping was started, and game slid into game. Billy took part in everything, but did not win first place as often as he had expected. An English writer beat him a dozen feet at tossing the caber. Jim Hazard beat him in putting the heavy "rock." Mark Hall out-jumped him standing and running. But at the standing high back-jump Billy did come first. Despite the handicap of his weight, this victory was due to his splendid back and abdominal lifting muscles. Saxon, very proud of her man boy, could not but see the admiration all had for him.

Nor did she prove in any way a social failure. When the tired and sweating players lay down in the dry sand

to cool off, she was persuaded into accompanying their
nonsense songs with the ukulélé. Nor was it long,
catching their spirit, ere she was singing to them and
teaching them quaint songs of early days which she had
herself learned as a little girl from Cady—Cady, the sa-
loonkeeper, pioneer, and ex-cavalryman, who had been
a bull-whacker on the Salt Lake Trail in the days before the railroad. One song which became an immediate
favorite was:

"Oh! times on Bitter Creek, they never can be
    beat,
Root hog or die is on every wagon sheet;
The sand within your throat, the dust within
    your eye,
Bend your back and stand it—root hog or die."

It was Mark Hall who brought up the matter of
Billy's challenge to race out the south wall of the cove,
though he referred to the test as lying somewhere in
the future. Billy surprised him by saying he was ready
at any time. Forthwith the crowd clamored for the
race. Hall offered to bet on himself, but there were no
takers. He offered two to one to Jim Hazard, who shook
his head and said he would accept three to one as a
sporting proposition. Billy heard and gritted his teeth.

"I'll take you for five dollars," he said to Hall, "but
not at those odds. I'll back myself even."

"It isn't your money I want; it's Hazard's," Hall
demurred. "Though I'll give either of you three to one."

"Even or nothing," Billy held out obstinately.

Hall finally closed both bets—even with Billy, and
three to one with Hazard.

The path along the knife-edge was so narrow that
it was impossible for runners to pass each other, so it

was arranged to time the men, Hall to go first and Billy to follow after an interval of half a minute.

Hall toed the mark and at the word was off with the form of a sprinter. Saxon's heart sank. She knew Billy had never crossed the stretch of sand at that speed. Billy darted forward thirty seconds later, and reached the foot of the rock when Hall was half way up. When both were on top and racing from notch to notch, the Iron Man announced that they had scaled the wall in the same time to a second.

"My money still looks good," Hazard remarked, "though I hope neither of them breaks a neck. I wouldn't take that run that way for all the gold that would fill the cove."

"But you'll take bigger chances swimming in a storm on Carmel Beach," his wife chided.

"Oh, I don't know," he retorted. "You haven't so far to fall when swimming."

Billy and Hall had disappeared and were making the circle around the end. Those on the beach were certain that the poet had gained in the dizzy spurts of flight along the knife-edge. Even Hazard admitted it.

"What price for my money now?" he cried excitedly, dancing up and down.

Hall had reappeared, the great jump accomplished, and was running shoreward. But there was no gap. Billy was on his heels, and on his heels he stayed, in to shore, down the wall, and to the mark on the beach. Billy had won by half a minute.

"Only by the watch," he panted. "Hall was over half a minute ahead of me out to the end. I'm not slower than I thought, but he's faster. He's a wooz of a sprinter. He could beat me ten times outa ten, except for accident. He was hung up at the jump by a

big sea. That's where I caught 'm. I jumped right after 'm on the same sea, then he set the pace home,
and all I had to do was take it."

"That's all right," said Hall. "You did better than
beat me. That's the first time in the history of Bierce's
Cove that two men made that jump on the same sea.
And all the risk was yours, coming last."

"It was a fluke," Billy insisted.

And at that point Saxon settled the dispute of mod-
esty and raised a general laugh by rippling chords on
the ukulélé and parodying an old hymn in negro min-
strel fashion:

> "De Lawd move in er mischievous way
> His blunders to perform."

Not until sunset did the merry crowd carry their
pots and pans and trove of mussels up to the road and
depart. Saxon and Billy watched them disappear, on
horses and behind horses, over the top of the first hill,
and then descended hand in hand through the thicket
to the camp. Billy threw himself on the sand and
stretched out.

"I don't know when I've been so tired," he yawned.
"An' there's one thing sure: I never had such a day.
It's worth livin' twenty years for an' then some."

He reached out his hand to Saxon, who lay beside
him.

"And, oh, I was so proud of you, Billy," she said.

"Huh, I want to say you was goin' some yourself.
They just took to you. Why, honest to God, Saxon,
in the singin' you was the whole show, along with the
ukulélé. All the women liked you, too, an' that's what
counts."

It was their first social triumph, and the taste of it
was sweet.

A little longer they lay in the warm sand. It was Billy who broke the silence, and what he said seemed to proceed out of profound meditation.

"Say, Saxon, d'ye know I don't care if I never see movin' pictures again."

Saxon and Billy were gone weeks on the trip south, but in the end they came back to Carmel. They had stopped with Hafler, the poet, in the Marble House, which he had built with his own hands. This queer dwelling was all in one room, built almost entirely of white marble. Hafler cooked, as over a campfire, in the huge marble fireplace, which he used in all ways as a kitchen. There were divers shelves of books, and the massive furniture he had made from redwood, as he had made the shakes for the roof. A blanket, stretched across a corner, gave Saxon privacy. The poet was on the verge of departing for San Francisco and New York, but remained a day over with them to explain the country and run over the government land with Billy. Saxon had wanted to go along that morning, but Hafler scornfully rejected her, telling her that her legs were too short. That night, when the men returned, Billy was played out to exhaustion. He frankly acknowledged that Hafler had walked him into the ground, and that his tongue had been hanging out from the first hour. Hafler estimated that they had covered fifty-five miles.

"But such miles!" Billy enlarged. "Half the time up or down, an' 'most all the time without trails. An' such a pace. He was dead right about your short legs, Saxon. You wouldn't a-lasted the first mile. An' such country! We ain't seen anything like it yet."

Hafler left the next day to catch the train at Monterey. He gave them the freedom of the Marble House, and told them to stay the whole winter if they wanted. Billy elected to loaf around and rest up that day. He was stiff and sore. Moreover, he was stunned by the exhibition of walking prowess on the part of the poet.

"Everybody can do something top-notch down in this country," he marveled. "Now take that Hafler. He's a bigger man than me, an' a heavier. An' weight's against walkin', too. But not with him. He's done eighty miles inside twenty-four hours, he told me, an' once a hundred an' seventy in three days. Why, he made a show outa me. I felt ashamed as a little kid."

"Remember, Billy," Saxon soothed him, "every man to his own game. And down here you're a top-notcher at *your* own game. There isn't one you're not the master of with the gloves."

"I guess that's right," he conceded. "But just the same it goes against the grain to be walked off my legs by a poet—by a *poet,* mind you."

They spent days in going over the government land, and in the end reluctantly decided against taking it up. The redwood canyons and great cliffs of the Santa Lucia Mountains fascinated Saxon; but she remembered what Hafler had told her of the summer fogs which hid the sun sometimes for a week or two at a time, and which lingered for months. Then, too, there was no access to market. It was many miles to where the nearest wagon road began, at Post's, and from there on, past Point Sur to Carmel, it was a weary and perilous way. Billy, with his teamster judgment, admitted that for heavy hauling it was anything but a picnic.

After they left Post's on the way back to Carmel, the condition of the road proved the wisdom of their rejection of the government land. They passed a rancher's wagon overturned, a second wagon with a broken axle, and the stage a hundred yards down the mountainside, where it had fallen, passengers, horses, road, and all.

"I guess they just about quit tryin' to use this road in the winter," Billy said. "It's horse-killin' an' man-killin', an' I can just see 'm freightin' that marble out over it I don't think."

From a financial standpoint, Saxon and Billy were putting aside much money. They paid no rent, their simple living was cheap, and Billy had all the work he cared to accept. The various members of the crowd seemed in a conspiracy to keep him busy. It was all odd jobs, but he preferred it so, for it enabled him to suit his time to Jim Hazard's. Each day they boxed and took a long swim through the surf. When Hazard finished his morning's writing, he would whoop through the pines to Billy, who dropped whatever work he was doing. After the swim, they would take a fresh shower at Hazard's house, rub each other down in training camp style, and be ready for the noon meal. In the afternoon Hazard returned to his desk, and Billy to his outdoor work, although, still later, they often met for a few miles' run over the hills. Training was a matter of habit to both men. Hazard, when he had finished with seven years of football, knowing the dire death that awaits the big-muscled athlete who ceases training abruptly, had been compelled to keep it up. Not only was it a necessity, but he had grown to like it. Billy also liked it, for he took great delight in the silk of his body.

Often, in the early morning, gun in hand, he was off with Mark Hall, who taught him to shoot and hunt. Hall had dragged a shotgun around from the days when he wore knee pants, and his keen observing eyes and knowledge of the habits of wild life were a revela-

tion to Billy. This part of the country was too settled
for large game, but Billy kept Saxon supplied with
squirrels and quail, cottontails and jackrabbits, snipe
and wild ducks. And they learned to eat roasted mallard and canvasback in the California style of sixteen
minutes in a hot oven. As he became expert with shotgun and rifle, he began to regret the deer and the mountain lion he had missed down below the Sur; and to
the requirements of the farm he and Saxon sought he
added plenty of game.

But it was not all play in Carmel. That portion
of the community which Saxon and Billy came to
know, "the crowd," was hard-working. Some worked
regularly, in the morning or late at night. Others
worked spasmodically, like the wild Irish playwright,
who would shut himself up for a week at a time,
then emerge, pale and drawn, to play like a mad-
man against the time of his next retirement. The pale
and youthful father of a family, with the face of
Shelley, who wrote vaudeville turns for a living and
blank verse tragedies and sonnet cycles for the despair
of managers and publishers, hid himself in a concrete
cell with three-foot walls, so piped, that, by turning
a lever, the whole structure spouted water upon the
impending intruder. But in the main, they respected
each other's work-time. They drifted into one another's
houses as the spirit prompted, but if they found a man
at work they went their way. This obtained to all except Mark Hall, who did not have to work for a living; and he climbed trees to get away from popularity
and compose in peace.

The crowd was unique in its democracy and soli-
darity. It had little intercourse with the sober and
conventional part of Carmel. This section constituted
the aristocracy of art and letters, and was sneered at
as bourgeois. In return, it looked askance at the crowd

with its rampant bohemianism. The taboo extended to Billy and Saxon. Billy took up the attitude of the clan and sought no work from the other camp. Nor was work offered him.

Hall kept open house. The big living room, with its huge fireplace, divans, shelves and tables of books and magazines, was the center of things. Here, Billy and Saxon were expected to be, and in truth found themselves to be, as much at home as anybody. Here, when wordy discussions on all subjects under the sun were not being waged, Billy played at cut-throat pedro, horrible fives, bridge, and pinochle. Saxon, a favorite of the young women, sewed with them, teaching them pretties and being taught in fair measure in return.

Billy took little interest in the many discussions waged in Hall's big living room. "Wind-chewin'," was his term for it. To him it was so much good time wasted that might be employed at a game of pedro, or going swimming, or wrestling in the sand. Saxon, on the contrary, delighted in the logomachy, though little enough she understood of it, following mainly by feeling, and once in a while catching a high light.

But what she could never comprehend was the pessimism that so often cropped up. The wild Irish playwright had terrible spells of depression. Shelley, who wrote vaudeville turns in the concrete cell, was a chronic pessimist. St. John, a young magazine writer, was an anarchic disciple of Nietzsche. Masson, a painter, held to a doctrine of eternal recurrence that was petrifying. And Hall, usually so merry, could outfoot them all when he once got started on the cosmic pathos of religion and the gibbering anthropomorphisms of those who loved not to die. At such times Saxon was oppressed by these sad children of art. It was inconceivable that they, of all people, should be so forlorn.

One night Hall turned suddenly upon Billy, who

had been following dimly and who only comprehended that to them everything in life was rotten and wrong.

"Here, you pagan, you, you stolid and flesh-fettered ox, you monstrosity of over-weening and perennial health and joy, what do you think of it?" Hall demanded.

"Oh, I've had my troubles," Billy answered, speaking in his wonted slow way. "I've had my hard times, an' fought a losin' strike, an' soaked my watch, an' ben unable to pay my rent or buy grub, an' slugged scabs, an' ben slugged, and ben thrown into jail for makin' a fool of myself. If I get you, I'd be a whole lot better to be a swell hog fattenin' for market an' nothin' worryin', than to be a guy sick to his stomach from not savvyin' how the world is made or from wonderin' what's the good of anything."

"That's good, that prize hog," the poet laughed. "Least irritation, least effort—a compromise of Nirvana and life. Least irritation, least effort, the ideal existence: a jellyfish floating in a tideless, tepid, twilight sea."

"But you're missin' all the good things," Billy objected.

"Name them," came the challenge.

Billy was silent a moment. To him life seemed a large and generous thing. He felt as if his arms ached from inability to compass it all, and he began, haltingly at first, to put his feeling into speech.

"If you'd ever stood up in the ring an' out-gamed an' out-fought a man as good as yourself for twenty rounds, you'd get what I'm drivin' at. Jim Hazard an' I get it when we swim out through the surf an' laugh in the teeth of the biggest breakers that ever pounded the beach, an' when we come out from the shower, rubbed down and dressed, our skin an' muscles like silk, our bodies an' brains all a'tinglin' like silk. . . ."

He paused and gave up from sheer inability to express ideas that were nebulous at best and that in reality were remembered sensations.

"Silk of the body, can you beat it?" he concluded lamely, feeling that he had failed to make his point, embarrassed by the circle of listeners.

"We know all that," Hall retorted. "The lies of the flesh. Afterward come rheumatism and diabetes. The wine of life is heady, but all too quickly it turns to——"

"Uric acid," interpolated the wild Irish playwright.

"They's plenty more of the good things," Billy took up with a sudden rush of words. "Good things all the way up from juicy porterhouse and the kind of coffee Mrs. Hall makes to. . . ." He hesitated at what he was about to say, then took it at a plunge. "To a woman you can love an' that loves you. Just take a look at Saxon there with the ukulélé in her lap. There's where I got the jellyfish in the dishwater an' the prize hog skinned to death."

A shout of applause and great hand-clapping went up from the girls, and Billy looked painfully uncomfortable.

"But suppose the silk goes out of your body till you creak like a rusty wheelbarrow?" Hall pursued. "Suppose, just suppose, Saxon went away with another man. What then?"

Billy considered a space.

"Then it'd be me for the dishwater an' the jellyfish, I guess." He straightened up in his chair and threw back his shoulders unconsciously as he ran a hand over his biceps and swelled it. Then he took another look at Saxon. "But thank the Lord I still got a wallop in both my arms an' a wife to fill 'em with love."

Again the girls applauded, and Mrs. Hall cried:

"Look at Saxon! She blushing! ——What have you to say for yourself?"

"That no woman could be happier," she stammered, "and no queen as proud. And that——"

She completed the thought by strumming on the ukulélé and singing:

"De Lawd move in er mischievous way
His blunders to perform."

"I give you best," Hall grinned to Billy.

"Oh, I don't know," Billy disclaimed modestly. "You've read so much I guess you know more about everything than I do."

"Oh! Oh!" "Traitor!" "Taking it all back!" the girls cried variously.

Billy took heart of courage, reassured them with a slow smile, and said:

"Just the same I'd sooner be myself than have book indigestion. An' as for Saxon, why, one kiss of her lips is worth more'n all the libraries in the world."

CARMEL ALFRESCO

Van Wyck Brooks

The young Van Wyck Brooks—who later carved a niche as one of America's foremost literary historians —left New York and came to Carmel in 1911. Here he was married and spent his honeymoon, before moving on to Palo Alto and a teaching job at Stanford University. The following, taken from his 1954 autobiographical *Scenes and Portraits: Memories of Childhood and Youth*, gives some personal appraisals of the artistic and literary life of the Peninsula. Brooks seems not to have been impressed by Carmel's inspirational qualities: "Others who had come from the East to write novels in this paradise found themselves becalmed and supine . . . turned into beachcombers, listlessly reading books they had read ten times before and searching the rocks for abalones."

———— >< <•> >< ————

I had only to see California to fall under the spell of it, beginning with the sunlight over the live-oak trees. It was February and at first I was puzzled by this light: why did it seem so magical, why so strange? Then I saw it was a winter sun shining over a summer scene, an entirely new combination to unaccustomed eyes. For I was used to so much greenery only under a summer sky; and, besides, how strange was this vegetation, the flowering mimosas, the manganita, the tangles of cactus, the palms, the eucalyptus. The fuchsias grew like shrubs in the gardens of Berkeley, where there were streets called "ways" on one of which Arthur Ryder lived, the friend of my childhood in Italy, now professor of Sanskrit. Carmel was a wildwood with an operatic setting where life itself also seemed half operatic and where curious dramas were taking place in the bungalows and cabins, smothered in blossoming vines, on the sylvan slope. There were sandy trails for streets, wandering through canyons carpeted with moss and with great white pines that caught the wind and shreds of the grey fog that swept in from the sea. There I was married in April, and I was to return there, three or four times at least, for many years.

In Carmel I spent several months before the college term began and I undertook to teach at Leland Stanford, living in the alfresco fashion that everybody practised on this quite romantic peninsula of Monterey. The wild past was still present there with even the remains of an outlaw's camp, the hut of Joaquin Murieta in the San José canyon, where Easter lilies grew as daisies grow elsewhere; and there was the forest scenery that Robert Louis Stevenson, after his visit, pictured in *Treasure Island*. There were the white-washed Mexican shanties of John Steinbeck's *Tortilla Flat* and the old adobe house where John Steinbeck himself was living when I returned to the peninsula later, one of those dwellings with Castilian roses covering the red-tiled roofs that survived from the old Spanish Mexican colonial times. If, moreover, one no longer saw the caballeros of the eighteen-forties with strings of bells on their embroidered pantaloons, Jaime de Angulo, with his Arab horse and his red sash and El Greco

beard, had all the look of a revenant from that earlier
time. This was the Spanish ethnologist-doctor who had
lived with the Indians in the Southwest, where he col-
lected the Indian tales that he was to put into final
form as a dying man forty years later on his mountain-
top ranch. There was never a figure more fantastic
than Jaime de Angulo came to be in those days when,
living alone, looking out at the Pacific, a decayed Don
Quixote, ragged and mad, he boxed with a pet stallion
and carved his meat with a great knife that hung from
his middle. But Carmel at all times abounded in every
sort of anomalous type,—for one, the old newspaper-
correspondent who conversed every night with the
people of Mars and had twelve typewritten volumes of
these conversations. George Sterling, the poet, who had
precisely the aspect of Dante in hell, a suicide later,
like his wife, haunted Point Lobos where the poetess
Nora French had leaped from the cliff; while others
who had come from the East to write novels in this
paradise found themselves there becalmed and supine.
They gave themselves over to day-dreams while their
minds ran down like clocks, as if they had lost the
keys to wind them up with, and they turned into beachcombers, listlessly reading books they had read ten
times before and searching the rocks for abalones. For
this Arcadia lay, one felt, outside the world in which
thought evolves and which came to seem insubstantial
in the bland sunny air.

I often felt in Carmel that I was immobilized, living
as if in a fresco of Puvis de Chavannes, for there was
something Theocritean, something Sicilian or Greek, in
this afternoon land of olive trees, honey-bees and
shepherds. There was also, down by the Big Sur, or,
rather, beyond on the coastal trail, a no man's country
as far as San Luis Obispo, a wilderness, sinister and
dark, where, supposedly, robbers dwelt, another

"Rogues' Harbour" like that of old Kentucky. One heard all manner of ominous tales of mysterious people hiding there, murderers who had escaped there, renegade whites and outcast Indians living in huts and caves, and the evil that seemed to brood over the region was all the stranger and more marked because of the splendid beauty of the mountainous coast. Even the lonely upland ranches that straggled by the road, northward from the Big Sur, overhanging the ocean, seemed somehow accursed or sad as one passed them on foot, as I did that first year on a three days' ramble, stopping at one ranch, for instance, where a tragic-looking woman was living quite alone with her steers and her sheep. At another ranch a burly bruiser with the look of a Mexican Brigham Young was riding with a troop of women, lashing his cattle. Long before Robinson Jeffers had published his poems about that coast one felt there a lurking possibility of monstrous things.

At that time I did not know Robinson Jeffers, nor do I remember on which of my visits to Carmel I began to see him, always at the same time on the ridge between Carmel and Monterey where the old trail through the pines joined the road. At four o'clock in the afternoon, invariably, if one happened to follow this trail, emerging from the woods on the brow of the hill,—where the gulf of Monterey appeared, suddenly, below,—there, overlooking the long slope with live-oaks scattered over it, Jeffers drove by in his old Ford. One could set one's watch by this coming of the poet in his brown tweed coat with his collar thrown back in the manner of Audubon or Byron, driving to Pacific Grove by way of Monterey. Then a few years later I used to see him on my walks around the Carmel point when he was building Tor House on the bluff above the dunes. He seemed to be always toiling up the cliff trail as I passed, with a boulder from the beach on his back, like Sisyphus; for, with only the occasional help of a mason, he set up this massive house himself with the tower that looked like a primitive Norman keep. Later he surrounded it with wild sweet alyssum, and a path of abalone shells led up from the gate. White pigeons circled round the tower, suggested perhaps by the white pigeons over the pueblo near Taos that had for him, no doubt, a special meaning.

For Jeffers, who looked like an Aztec with his slate-grey heavy-lidded eyes that reminded one of the eyes of an old tortoise, lived in the Stone Age, mentally, in a sort of historical vacuum, and seemed to be naturally drawn to the prehistoric. He surrounded himself with mementos of this like the rock-pile resembling a cromlech that he built behind the house. In one of his poems he saw all history as a "rotted floor" sagging under man's foot, and for him humanity was simply "the mould to break away from," while, with no concern for the living world, his mind harked back to primordial times before men were obsessed with the illusions of philanthropy and progress. I remember the pleasure with which he pointed out to me that the stones in the walls of a big house near by were laid as they were in King Arthur's castle of Tintagel. But even that period was late for him; and, wholly removed as his mind was from the modern human world, he would have felt more at home in the circle at Stonehenge. America did not exist for him, its towns or people, its literary life, even the best poets of his own time, and he and his wife on their travels always went to the British Isles, or, rather, the small islands surrounding Ireland and Scotland. They knew all of these, the Arran isles, the Orkneys and the Shetlands, where they found ruins and where they loved the fog, for they were "angry with the sun" that overpowered them at home,—to quote another phrase from Jeff-

ers's poems. There they found old whalebones too,
bleached driftwood and the fossils that took them back
before the time of man, feeding the poet's fantasy of
the prehistoric. No humanistic mind could sympathize
with Jeffers's nihilistic point of view, but, for all its
bleakness, there was no doubt of the real grandeur of
feeling or of the elevation that marked his poems.

As a matter of fact, antipathetic as the burden of
his work might be, this poet was destined to survive
many changes of fashion. Pointedly ignored in years
to come in the dominant critical circles, he possessed
an integrity that weathered both attacks and silence,
an unmistakable indivisible unity and wholeness of belief and mood that one finds in very few writers in
any generation. Yet how deadly to the human sense
was this belief in violence, which had been, as he said,
"the sire of all the world's values" and which led him
to choose for an emblem the hawk,—he named his
"Hawk Tower" after it,—that one saw constantly
poised over Point Lobos. Accepting Spengler's eternal recurrence of otherwise meaningless culture-cycles,
he defended primitive barbarity as the fate of man-
kind, seeing it as quite good enough for the species he
despised with his own active neo-Calvinism. For he
was the true child of his father, the theological professor who had taught him to read Greek when he was
five, so that Æschylus and Sophocles were also in his
blood along with the predestinationism of Jonathan
Edwards. While his people were "all compelled, all un-
happy, all helpless," a phrase that one found in
Thurso's Landing, they were also, on the whole, "vipers"
and justly damned; and this drew Jeffers tempera-
mentally to the leaders of the Fascists for whom men
were inferior animals to be driven with whips. But
I often wondered why he took the Spanish civil war
so hard that after it he seldom wrote again. He was

evidently confused by this, and it struck me that perhaps, admiring the hawk for so many years, he had never previously watched the hawk really in action. For this defender of the bird of prey was the most humane of men who had never himself killed either bird or beast.

What was it in the Carmel atmosphere that so conduced to violence?—for Jeffers's themes had usually a basis in fact there. I almost witnessed a murder, for instance, that reappeared in a poem of his. It was committed at night in a shack in a eucalyptus grove where a Mexican woman with a Cuban husband stabbed her lover, a Filipino, and thrust the body into an oven outside. The crime was clumsily gruesome enough and brutally careless as well, for a passer-by saw the body in the early morning while the murderers were found, asleep and indifferent, within; and although I had not seen the crime, I saw the child who witnessed it, the daughter of the Mexican woman who was present in the shack. With eyes that seemed permanently frightened, she kept the gate for a number of years at the lodge of a wild park not far away. But nihilism too was endemic in Carmel, like suicide and murder and along with the Mediterranean beauty of the scene; and it seemed the right place for Henry Miller to say that "it doesn't matter a damn whether the world is going to the dogs or not."

SEASONS IN CARMEL

George Sterling

At the center of the Carmel bohemia that flourished during the first two decades of the twentieth century was George Sterling—poet, dramatist, and critic. He was born in 1865 in Sag Harbor, New York. As a young man he came West and took a job in a real estate office owned by an uncle in Oakland, writing verse on the side and developing strong friendships with Jack London, Ambrose Bierce, and other writers and artists of the Bay Area. Encouraged by Bierce to devote full time to writing, Sterling gave up real estate and settled in Carmel where, in Mary Austin's words, he "was easily the most arresting figure." As arresting as he was—his resemblance to Dante was striking—time has not dealt kindly with his literary output. He did write some memorable sonnets and poems (two of which are included here), as well as a perceptive book about Robinson Jeffers, but he is probably best remembered today as the originator of the "Abalone Song," a doggerel verse-chant that was to be sung while pounding the tough flesh of the abalone. Jack London incorporated several stanzas of the song in his Carmel section of *Valley of the Moon*, where Sterling appears as the character Mark Hall.

Some stick to biz, some flirt with Liz
Down on the sands of Coney;

131

But we, by hell, stay in Carmel,
　And whang the abalone.

Sterling committed suicide in San Francisco in 1926.

———◆—◀◆▶—◆———

Spring In Carmel

O'er Carmel fields in the springtime the sea-gulls
　　follow the plow.
White, white wings on the blue above!
White were your brow and breast, O Love!
　But I cannot see you now.
Tireless ever the Mission swallow
Dips to meadow and poppied hollow;
Well for her mate that he can follow,
　As the buds are on the bough.

By the woods and waters of Carmel the lark is
　　glad in the sun.
Harrow! harrow! music of God!
Near to your nest her feet have trod,
　Whose journeyings are done.
Sing, O lover! I cannot sing.
Wild and sad are the thoughts you bring.
Well for you are the skies of spring,
　And to me all skies are one.

In the beautiful woods of Carmel an iris bends to
　　the wind.
O thou far-off and sorrowful flower!
Rose that I found in a tragic hour!
　Rose that I shall not find!
Petals that fell so soft and slowly,
Fragrant snows on the grasses lowly,
Gathered now would I call you holy
　Ever to eyes once blind.

In the pine-sweet valley of Carmel the cream-cups
    scatter in foam.
Azures of early lupin there!
Now the wild lilac floods the air
  Like a broken honey-comb.
So could the flowers of Paradise
Pour their souls to the morning skies;
So like a ghost your fragrance lies.
  On the path that once led home.

On the emerald hills of Carmel the spring and
    winter have met.
Here I find in a gentled spot
The frost of the wild forget-me-not,
  And—I cannot forget.
Heart once light as the floating feather
Borne aloft in the sunny weather,
Spring and winter have come together—
  Shall you and she meet yet?

On the rocks and beaches of Carmel the surf is
    mighty to-day.
Breaker and lifting billow call
To the high, blue Silence over all
  With the word no heart can say.
Time-to-be, shall I hear it ever?
Time-that-is, with the hands that sever,
Cry all words but the dreadful "Never!"
  And name of her far away!

------◦◦◦◀◦◦------

Autumn In Carmel

Now with a sigh November comes to the brood-
    ing land.

Yellowing now toward winter the willows of Carmel stand.
Under the pine her needles lie redder with the rain.
Gipsy birds from the northland visit our woods
again.

Hunters wait on the hillside, watching the plow-
man pass
And the red hawk's shadow gliding over the new-
born grass.
Purple and white the sea-gulls swarm at the river-
mouth.
Pearl of mutable heavens towers upon the south.

Westward pine and cypress stand in a sadder
light.
Flocks of the veering curlew flash for an instant
white,
Wreaths of the mallard, shifting, melt on the vacant blue.
Over the hard horizon dreams are calling anew.

Dumb with the sense of wonder hidden from hand
and eye,—
Wistful yet for the Secret ocean and earth deny,—
Baffled for Beauty's haunting, hearts are peaceless
to-day,
Seeing the dusk of sapphire deepen within the
bay.

Far on the kelp the heron stands for awhile at
rest.
The lichen-colored breaker hollows a leaning
breast.
Desolate, hard and tawny, the sands lie clean and
wide,

Dry with the wafted sea-wind, wet with the fallen
     tide.

Early the autumn sunset tinges to mauve the foam;
Shyly the rabbit, feeding, crosses the road to
     home.
Daylight, lingering golden, touches the tallest tree,
Ere the rain, like silver harp-strings, comes slant-
     ing in from sea.

JEFFERS

Lawrence Clark Powell

Robinson Jeffers and his wife, Una, came to Carmel in 1914. They settled on a large plot of land at Carmel Point, where Jeffers built a house and tower out of granite and for the next forty years wrote poems and verse plays that slowly brought him recognition as one of America's greatest poets. He never joined the Carmel literary "crowd" and over the years earned a reputation as a brooding recluse. The creator of those often violent and pessimistic poems seems an unlikely person to have sat on the sand pounding shellfish to the rhythms of George Sterling's "Abalone Song." Lawrence Clark Powell visited Jeffers in 1929, and wrote a book about him which was published in 1934. In the essay that follows Powell draws not only on personal acquaintance but on his own deep affinity for the California landscape and the way in which it has influenced not only Jeffers, but other California writers, too. Powell is former head librarian and dean of the library school at U.C.L.A. He now lives in Phoenix where he teaches and writes.

***

California's Big Sur coast had a long wait for its laureate.

Nearly four centuries elapsed between the time its first discoverer, Juan Rodriguez Cabrillo, saw it from a ship at sea and when its ultimate poet, Robinson Jeffers, saw it from a stagecoach on land.

Cabrillo wrote in his log: "All the coast passed this day is very bold; there is a great swell and the land is very high. There are mountains which seem to reach the heavens, and the sea beats on them; sailing along close to land, it appears as though they would fall on the ships."

Jeffers wrote to his publisher, after a plan to take his bride of a year and live in Europe was aborted by the war: "The August [1914] news turned us to this village of Carmel instead, and when the stagecoach topped the hill from Monterey, and we looked down through pines and seafog on Carmel Bay, it was evident that we had come without knowing it to our inevitable place."

In the time between Cabrillo and Jeffers others had come, seen, stayed briefly, written, and left. Dana was excited by the social life of Monterey in the 1830s. Robert Louis Stevenson was too ill to venture very far beyond the Carmel Mission. A camping trip into the nearby Santa Lucia mountains nearly killed him. He managed nevertheless to write a few essays about the region which are timelessly true. If Mary Austin had remained and been less egocentric, she might have done for the region what her *Land of Little Rain* did for the country east of the Sierra Nevada. She left a few years before Jeffers came, never to return. George Sterling's gifts were not equal to the grandeur of the coast, although he did write one memorable poem to the abalone. His death in 1926 was commemorated by Jeffers in a moving elegy.

Now, in 1968, we can look back over the more than half century since Robinson Jeffers first saw the coast at Carmel and recognize the inevitability of his becoming the poet laureate of the region. Everything conspired to make it so. He was young—only twenty-seven —and physically powerful; he was passionately wedded to a woman of great beauty and intense nature; he was highly educated in travel, classics, literature and science; he was a poet from boyhood and youth in Europe and southern California; and, as fully important as the rest, he enjoyed a small regular income, which afforded the leisure needed for writing something other than journalism. Poetry written on an empty stomach is lean food for readers.

In 1914 Carmel was indeed a village. South to the Big Sur the coast was still as Cabrillo first saw it. A rough wagon road lurched as far as the canyon of the Big Sur River. Beyond that there was a horse trail only, high above the great cliffs.

Then it was that the time, the place and the poet coalesced in one of those unique conjunctions that produces literature. With poem after poem, book upon book, Robinson Jeffers built his lasting monument, from *Californians* in 1916 to *The Beginning and the End,* published in 1963, a year after his death at the age of seventy-five. In this half century of achievement he rose to supreme eminence, a Shasta among poets. No other bard of his time, other than Yeats, approached the power and the glory, the strength and the tenderness, or the prophetic vision of Jeffers. He towered too high for most to see the full bulk of him. Only now are we beginning to perceive him in perspective.

Until he entered the magnetic field that was to hold him in Carmel until his death, Jeffers' future was cloudy and uncertain. His father, an eminent theologian, had hopes for his son to become a professional man, a minister or a doctor. His younger brother, Hamilton, was an astronomer at the University of California's Lick Observatory.

Robinson graduated from Occidental College in 1905, then studied medicine at the University of Southern California, although he never completed the M.D. At both schools he contributed poetry to the student magazines. He also wrestled and was on the track team, and climbed the best southern California had to offer in the way of mountains: Baldy and Grayback. He resembled other young bohemians then and now, given to wine, women and sports. The poems he wrote of nature and love were conventional.

Then, in a German class at U.S.C., he met his fate in a glance, just as Stevenson met his when he first saw Fanny Osbourne. It was an encounter as decisive as the subsequent one with the coast at Carmel. Jeffers' fate was a woman, a woman in her early twenties, taking her M.A. in English. "She was very beautiful," Jeffers recalled years later, "capable of intense joy and passionate resentment, little of stature, dowered with great blue eyes and heavy bronze hair. It was no wonder that she was married at seventeen."

Una Call Kuster was indeed a married woman, and there ensued several years of troublesome and passionate occasions, including a trial separation, before her husband granted her a divorce. Robin and Una were married at Tacoma in 1913. Their children were twin sons, Donnan and Garth, born three years later—and his poems.

"My nature is cold and undiscriminating," Jeffers wrote, "she excited and focused it, gave it eyes and nerves and sympathies. She never saw any of my poems until they were finished and typed, and yet by her presence and conversation she has co-authored every one of them. She is more like a woman in a Scotch ballad, passionate, untamed, and rather heroic—or like a falcon—than like any ordinary person."

The Jeffers lived first in a cabin in the Carmel pinewood. Then in 1919 they bought land on Mission Point, south of the village, and there built a stone house. Because the mason needed a helper, Jeffers worked in this role at $4.00 a day. Thus his fingers learned the art, he was to say later, of marrying stone with stone. He went on alone to build Hawk Tower, also of the local sea granite, and to plant a forest of several thousand cypress and eucalyptus trees, for privacy and protection from the sea wind.

House and tower stand to this day. All but a few of the trees, however, have been felled to make room for houses on the land the Jeffers were eventually forced to sell to pay rising taxes and assessments. Hindsight enables us to see what an unusual state park could have been made of the original acreage, trees, house and tower. The timing was wrong. Now it is too late. The only thing Time has not touched is the poetry. Jeffers knew full well what he had wrought: "a few poems stuck in the world's thought."

Anyone writing of great poetry is confronted at last by mystery. This is true of Jeffers' work. We can say that it was the fruit of his double marriage, to a woman and to a land, that it was fertilized by his heritage and education; and yet we do not know what were the precise or the subtle things that transformed him from a good poet to a great poet.

His first book, *Flagons and Apples,* published at Los Angeles in 1912, sponsored by John Steven McGroarty, the Mission Play poet, is composed of conventional love lyrics, written mostly to Una in the years of their stormy courtship. His second book, *Californians,* contains transitional nature poetry, with both southern California and Big Sur settings. Healed of his lovesickness, Jeffers turned outward to the splendors of the natural world and to write objective narratives, often on tragic themes. The form and the diction

of his verse remained traditional, and the influence of
Milton, Wordsworth and Shelley is omnipresent.

Eight years passed before his third book, *Tamar and
Other Poems,* lit the heavens like a sun. His verse was
no longer conventional in form, diction, or subject.
Sex had become a major theme. His voice was prophetic, his world view somber. Critics were moved to high
praise. Readers were attracted. Publishers bid for him.
He became famous as a poet, legendary as a recluse.

What happened in those eight years to effect these
radical changes? Here is the mystery, one similar to the
transformation of Walt Whitman from hack journalist
to the author of *Leaves of Grass.* Jeffers himself seemed
puzzled by the change. In writing of the year 1917
he said, "Great men have done their work before they
were thirty, but I wasn't born yet."

Was it the war that destroyed his inherited Christian idealism? Was it the death of his father and the
birth of his sons, which occurred in 1916? The building of Tor House in 1919? Could it have been an emotional experience outside of marriage? From the beginning Una held him on a choke-tight rein. He was
attractive to women. Described as a Greek god in
youth, he aged nobly, illustrating the truth of his
verse, "The heads of strong old age are beautiful beyond all grace of youth; they have dealt with life and
been atempered by it."

Clues to the mystery are found throughout his work.
In 1938, after he and Una had weathered a terrible
crisis in their marriage, involving another woman, and
he found himself exhausted and temporarily written
out, Jeffers wrote an anguished letter to Una: "I believe I'll have a new birth in the course of time—not
willing yet to grow old at fifty like Wordsworth, and
survive myself—something will happen—and *live*

through this hell come home to me—something will change, something will happen.

"It is a little like my extravagances of 1917 to '19, except that I was uncritical then, and able to keep myself fairly quiet by not writing a lot of foolishness. (Now I know too much). After that we began to make Tor House—*and that was worth while,*—quite aside from the accidental birth of my own mind."

A strange letter, both revealing and concealing. Among the 400 letters in the [Ann N.] Ridgeway volume [*Selected Letters of Robinson Jeffers*], it is the only one that is not crystal clear. It was obviously written under intense emotional stress.

Another clue to Jeffers' miraculous maturity is found in the introduction he wrote for the Modern Library edition of *Roan Stallion, Tamar, and Other Poems* (1935), in which he tells of his wish to become original and yet not be eccentric, and of meditating on his literary future one day in 1914 on a walk he and Una took in the Carmel pinewood:

"The seafog was coming up the ravine, fingering through the pines, the air smelled of the sea and pine-resin and yerba buena, my girl and my dog were with me . . . and I was standing there like a poor God-forsaken man-of-letters, making my final decision not to become a 'modern.' I did not want to become slight and fantastic, abstract and unintelligible.

"I was doomed to go on imitating dead men, unless some impossible wind should blow me emotions or ideas, or a point of view, or even mere rhythms that had not occurred to them. This book began to be written three or four years later. I was past my greensickness by that time, and did not stop to think whether the verses were original or followed a tendency, or would find a reader. Nor have I ever considered whether they deserved to find one."

A reading of the newly published Jeffers letters reveals the ambivalent feelings he had about the isolation from society and rigid work schedule Una held him to—writing in the morning, stonework and tree planting and watering in the afternoon. He had a gregarious side to this nature and a magnetism for women, both of which were threats to his creative routine and which Una ruthlessly curbed.

Consider this confession by Jeffers, in a review he wrote of a fellow poet's book:

"A poet is a specialist highly developed in some few issues and deficient or at least repressed in others; the energy that informs this book will perhaps not content itself with words and ideas. These are something, but they are such a little part of life;—as if a lover should be satisfied with fondling the hair or admiring the hands. Strong natures do not willingly concentrate on poetry, they need some exile or blindness to shut them up to it." Jeffers had Una.

Now is it clear what brought this poet to genius? Not altogether, at least not to me.

What *is* clear is that from 1924 to 1933 Jeffers' creative arc rose to zenith in a fiery trajectory of great books that established his lasting fame. *Tamar, Roan Stallion, The Women at Point Sur, Cawdor, Dear Judas, The Loving Shepherdess, Thurso's Landing* and, finally, the volume *Give Your Heart to the Hawks.* In the long narratives and short lyrics, which comprise these volumes of his prime, we find the poet at his finest.

Other books followed, including more narratives and lyrics, and the Broadway triumph of *Medea,* his adaptation of Euripides, actually more Judith Anderson than Jeffers. The money it earned was sorely needed. Among other expenses, the Jefferses were assessed $6,000 for a sewer district they had no need for.

History dealt roughly with Jeffers. The Second World War was shattering. As a strong, young man he survived the shock of the first, but the conflict that began in 1939 hit him at age 50, and he never recovered from it. His tragic view of humanity deepened, as he saw civilization destroying itself. The atomic bomb was the final blow. His last verses, except for a few tender family pieces, are bleak and often strident with prosaic reiterations of his doomful philosophy.

To add to his metaphysical sorrow, personal grief became nearly unbearable with the death of Una from cancer in 1950. Their life had been lived upon the assumption that she would survive him, to write his biography. It would have been a great one, for Una Jeffers was a gifted writer. Her letters pulse with life. Robin bore her death like the stoic he was. He survived her by a dozen years, lovingly cared for by Donnan and his wife Lee, comforted with grandchildren by them, and by Garth and his German wife. It was nevertheless a kind of death in life. To compound misery his publisher neglected his books and the new generation of academic critics scorned his verse.

When I wrote my thesis on Robinson Jeffers, as a student in France nearly 40 years ago, I had been on the Big Sur coast only once, in 1929, at the time the Jeffers family was in Ireland, and then only for a week; and yet it was long enough for me to see and to sense the inseparable relationship between his poetry and the landscape. My eventual book on Jeffers included a map of the coast, showing the settings of his poems, drawn by M.F.K. Fisher, a fellow student in Dijon.

Upon my return to California I visited the Jeffers for

the first time. It was a thrilling experience for me, a very young man at the threshold of a literary career, and their kindness and encouragement were decisive and helpful. The visit resulted in my first contribution to *Westways Magazine* [March, 1934], an article entitled "Robinson Jeffers on Life and Letters."

Robin and Una drove me down coast as far as the road then went, to a point beyond the canyon of the Big Sur River. There were books and maps in the car with us, and many a sudden stop for animated discussion. As a result, the American edition of my book contained a fuller map, drawn by Ward Ritchie, and which has since served literary pilgrims to the Jeffers country.

I too have returned time and again to that enchanted coast, always with a volume of Jeffers on the seat beside me. His poetry is moving wherever it is read, but read there in the setting which it exalts, it is supremely so. However high his soaring vision takes us—and 50 years ago Jeffers foresaw our colonization of outer space—his poetry remains rooted in earth. He viewed the coast and the mountains with the eyes of a trained scientist. His work can be read with joyful recognition by botanist, ornithologist, geologist, meteorologist and astronomer. Flowers and trees, birds, rocks, weather, the stars, all are woven into the texture of his verse, giving it an intense reality.

Thanks to such citizens as architect Nathanael Owings and his wife Margaret, writer Nicholas Roosevelt and State Senator Fred Farr, the coast road, State 1, was declared a Scenic Highway and the zealots in Sacramento restrained from widening it. The road *is* narrow, winding, precipitous, most certainly hazardous, and in storm impassable. Let it remain so, world without end. Our faraway discoverer would not be dishonored if it were to be renamed the Cabrillo-Jeffers Highway.

As for the way in which Tor House and Hawk Tower have been surrounded by Carmel's flooding expansion, Jeffers took the long view of the visionary poet, seeing far beyond the ultimate disappearance of his handiwork. Here is what he wrote in the poem "Tor House":

> But if you should look in your idleness after ten
> thousand years,
> It is the granite knoll on the granite
> And lava tongue in the midst of the bay, by the
> mouth of the Carmel
> River-valley, these four will remain
> In the change of names.

And the poem "Post-Mortem" ends with these poignant lines:

> Though one at the end of the age and far off
> from this place
> Should meet my presence in a poem,
> The ghost would not care but be here, long sunset
> shadow in the seams of the granite, and forgotten,
> The flesh, a spirit for the stone.

BOATS IN A FOG

Robinson Jeffers

Sports and gallantries, the stage, the arts, the antics of
    dancers,
The exuberant voices of music,
Have charm for children but lack nobility; it is bitter
    earnestness
That makes beauty; the mind
Knows, grown adult.

                A sudden fog-drift muffled the
                ocean,
A throbbing of engines moved in it,
At length, a stone's throw out, between the rocks and
    the vapor,
One by one moved shadows
Out of the mystery, shadows, fishing-boats, trailing
    each other
Following the cliff for guidance,
Holding a difficult path between the peril of the sea-
    fog
And the foam on the shore granite.
One by one, trailing their leader, six crept by me,
Out of the vapor and into it,
The throb of their engines subdued by the fog, patient
    and cautious,

Coasting all round the peninsula
Back to the buoys in Monterey harbor. A flight of peli-
  cans
Is nothing lovelier to look at;
The flight of the planets is nothing nobler; all the arts
  lose virtue
Against the essential reality
Of creatures going about their business among the
  equally
Earnest elements of nature.

HANDS

Robinson Jeffers

Inside a cave in a narrow canyon near Tassajara
The vault of rock is painted with hands,
A multitude of hands in the twilight, a cloud of men's
   palms, no more,
No other picture. There's no one to say
Whether the brown shy quiet people who are dead in-
   tended
Religion or magic, or made their tracings
In the idleness of art; but over the division of years
   these careful
Signs-manual are now like a sealed message
Saying: "Look: we also were human; we had hands,
   not paws. All hail
You people with the cleverer hands, our supplanters
In the beautiful country; enjoy her a season, her beauty,
   and come down
And be supplanted; for you also are human."

CANNERY ROW

John Steinbeck

The late John Steinbeck's *Cannery Row* (1945) and its sequel *Sweet Thursday* (1954) are two of the finest, funniest books ever to come out of California soil—coastal or inland. Both novels are set largely in Monterey's old cannery district which, by the time *Cannery Row* was written, were starting to shut down because of the sardine shortage brought on by over-fishing. Steinbeck presents an exotic, outrageous, and wonderful group of characters—Doc, Mack, Hazel, Lee Chong, the boys of the Palace Flophouse, the girls of the Bear Flag. The settings, from the vacant lots and back streets of Monterey to the coastal tidepools and Carmel backcountry, are authentic. The characters, many of them at least, were based on Steinbeck's own friends and cronies. The Cannery Row that Steinbeck depicts, however, would hardly be recognized by most of his characters today. The Row is now a respectable tourist trap—a street of gift shops, art galleries, and fancy seafood restaurants.

━━━━━━━━━━━━━━

Cannery Row in Monterey in California is a poem, a stink, a grating noise, a quality of light, a tone, a habit, a nostalgia, a dream. Cannery Row is the gathered and scattered, tin and iron and rust and splintered

wood, chipped pavement and weedy lots and junk
heaps, sardine canneries of corrugated iron, honky
tonks, restaurants and whore houses, and little crowded
groceries, and laboratories and flophouses. Its inhabitants are, as the man once said, "whores, pimps, gam-
blers, and sons of bitches," by which he meant Everybody. Had the man looked through another peephole
he might have said, "Saints and angels and martyrs and
holy men," and he would have meant the same thing.

In the morning when the sardine fleet has made a
catch, the purse-seiners waddle heavily into the bay
blowing their whistles. The deep-laden boats pull in
against the coast where the canneries dip their tails into the bay. The figure is advisedly chosen, for if the
canneries dipped their mouths into the bay the canned
sardines which emerge from the other end would be
metaphorically, at least, even more horrifying. Then
cannery whistles scream and all over the town men
and women scramble into their clothes and come running down to the Row to go to work. Then shining
cars bring the upper classes down: superintendents,
accountants, owners who disappear into offices. Then
from the town pour Wops and Chinamen and Polaks,
men and women in trousers and rubber coats and oil-
cloth aprons. They come running to clean and cut and
pack and cook and can the fish. The whole street
rumbles and groans and screams and rattles while the
silver rivers of fish pour in out of the boats and the
boats rise higher and higher in the water until they are
empty. The canneries rumble and rattle and squeak
until the last fish is cleaned and cut and cooked and
canned and then the whistles scream again and the
dripping, smelly, tired Wops and Chinamen and Polaks,
men and women, straggle out and droop their ways up
the hill into the town and Cannery Row becomes itself
again—quiet and magical. Its normal life returns. The

bums who retired in disgust under the black cypress
tree come out to sit on the rusty pipes in the vacant
lot. The girls from Dora's emerge for a bit of sun if
there is any. Doc strolls from the Western Biological
Laboratory and crosses the street to Lee Chong's grocery for two quarts of beer. Henri the painter noses
like an Airedale through the junk in the grass-grown
lot for some part or piece of wood or metal he needs
for the boat he is building. Then the darkness edges in
and the street light comes on in front of Dora's—the
lamp which makes perpetual moonlight in Cannery
Row. Callers arrive at Western Biological to see Doc,
and he crosses the street to Lee Chong's for five quarts
of beer.

Doc was collecting marine animals in the Great Tide
Pool on the tip of the Peninsula. It is a fabulous place:
when the tide is in, a wave-churned basin, creamy with
foam, whipped by the combers that roll in from the
whistling buoy on the reef. But when the tide goes out
the little water world becomes quiet and lovely. The
sea is very clear and the bottom becomes fantastic with
hurrying, fighting, feeding, breeding animals. Crabs
rush from frond to frond of the waving algae. Starfish
squat over mussels and limpets, attach their million
little suckers and then slowly lift with incredible power
until the prey is broken from the rock. And then the
starfish stomach comes out and envelops its food. Or-
ange and speckled and fluted nudibranchs slide grace-
fully over the rocks, their skirts waving like the dresses
of Spanish dancers. And black eels poke their heads
out of crevices and wait for prey. The snapping shrimps
with their trigger claws pop loudly. The lovely, colored
world is glassed over. Hermit crabs like frantic children

scamper on the bottom sand. And now one, finding an empty snail shell he likes better than his own, creeps out, exposing his soft body to the enemy for a moment, and then pops into the new shell. A wave breaks over the barrier, and churns the glassy water for a moment and mixes bubbles into the pool, and then it clears and is tranquil and lovely and murderous again. Here a crab tears a leg from his brother. The anemones expand like soft and brilliant flowers, inviting any tired and perplexed animal to lie for a moment in their arms, and when some small crab or little tide-pool Johnnie accepts the green and purple invitation, the petals whip in, the stinging cells shoot tiny narcotic needles into the prey and it grows weak and perhaps sleepy while the searing caustic digestive acids melt its body down.

Then the creeping murderer, the octopus, steals out, slowly, softly, moving like a gray mist, pretending now to be a bit of weed, now a rock, now a lump of decaying meat while its evil goat eyes watch coldly. It oozes and flows toward a feeding crab, and as it comes close its yellow eyes burn and its body turns rosy with the pulsing color of anticipation and rage. Then suddenly it runs lightly on the tips of its arms, as ferociously as a charging cat. It leaps savagely on the crab, there is a puff of black fluid, and the struggling mass is obscured in the sepia cloud while the octopus murders the crab. On the exposed rocks out of the water, the barnacles bubble behind their closed doors and the limpets dry out. And down to the rocks come the black flies to eat anything they can find. The sharp smell of iodine from the algae, and the lime smell of calcareous bodies and the smell of powerful protean, smell of sperm and ova fill the air. On the exposed rocks the starfish emit semen and eggs from between their rays. The smells of life and richness, of death and digestion,

of decay and birth, burden the air. And salt spray
blows in from the barrier where the ocean waits for its
rising-tide strength to permit it back into the Great Tide
Pool again. And on the reef the whistling buoy bellows
like a sad and patient bull.

Monterey is a city with a long and brilliant literary
tradition. It remembers with pleasure and some glory
that Robert Louis Stevenson lived there. Treasure
Island certainly has the topography and the coastal plan
of Pt. Lobos. More recently in Carmel there have been
a great number of literary men about, but there is not
the old flavor, the old dignity of the true belles-lettres.
Once the town was greatly outraged over what the citizens considered a slight to an author. It had to do
with the death of Josh Billings, the great humorist.

Where the new postoffice is, there used to be a deep
gulch with water flowing in it and a little foot
bridge over it. On one side of the gulch was a fine old
adobe and on the other the house of the doctor who
handled all the sickness, birth, and death in the town.
He worked with animals too and, having studied in
France, he even dabbled in the new practice of em-
balming bodies before they were buried. Some of the
oldtimers considered this sentimental and some thought
it wasteful and to some it was sacrilegious since there
was no provision for it in any sacred volume. But
the better and richer families were coming to it and it
looked to become a fad.

One morning elderly Mr. Carriaga was walking from
his house on the hill down toward Alvarado Street.
He was just crossing the foot bridge when his attention
was drawn to a small boy and a dog struggling up out
of the gulch. The boy carried a liver while the dog

dragged yards of intestine at the end of which a stomach dangled. Mr. Carriaga paused and addressed the little boy politely: "Good morning."

In those days little boys were courteous. "Good morning, sir."

"Where are you going with the liver?"

"I'm going to make some chum and catch some mackerel."

Mr. Carriaga smiled. "And the dog, will he catch mackerel too?"

"The dog found that. It's his, sir. We found them in the gulch."

Mr. Carriaga smiled and strolled on and then his mind began to work. That isn't a beef liver, it's too small. And it isn't a calf's liver, it's too red. It isn't a sheep's liver—Now his mind was alert. At the corner he met Mr. Ryan.

"Anyone die in Monterey last night?" he asked.

"Not that I know of," said Mr. Ryan.

"Anyone killed?"

"No."

They walked on together and Mr. Carriaga told about the little boy and the dog.

At the Adobe Bar a number of citizens were gathered for their morning conversation. There Mr. Carriaga told his story again and he had just finished when the constable came into the Adobe. He should know if anyone had died. "No one died in Monterey," he said. "But Josh Billings died out at the Hotel del Monte."

The men in the bar were silent. And the same thought went through all their minds. Josh Billings was a great man, a great writer. He had honored Monterey by dying there and he had been degraded. Without much discussion a committee formed made up of everyone there. The stern men walked quickly to the gulch and across the foot bridge and they hammered on the door of the doctor who had studied in France.

He had worked late. The knocking got him out of bed and brought him tousled of hair and beard to the door in his nightgown. Mr. Carriaga addressed him sternly: "Did you embalm Josh Billings?"

"Why—yes."

"What did you do with his tripas?"

"Why—I threw them in the gulch where I always do."

They made him dress quickly then and they hurried down to the beach. If the little boy had gone quickly about his business, it would have been too late. He was just getting into a boat when the committee arrived. The intestine was in the sand where the dog had abandoned it.

Then the French doctor was made to collect the parts. He was forced to wash them reverently and pick out as much sand as possible. The doctor himself had to stand the expense of the leaden box which went into the coffin of Josh Billings. For Monterey was not a town to let dishonor come to a literary man.

Early morning is a time of magic in Cannery Row. In the gray time after the light has come and before the sun has risen, the Row seems to hang suspended out of time in a silvery light. The street lights go out, and the weeds are a brilliant green. The corrugated iron of the canneries glows with the pearly lucence of platinum or old pewter. No automobiles are running then. The street is silent of progress and business. And the rush and drag of the waves can be heard as they splash in among the piles of the canneries. It is a time of great peace, a deserted time, a little era of rest. Cats drip over the fences and slither like syrup over the ground to look for fish heads. Silent early morning dogs parade majestically picking and choosing judiciously whereon to pee. The sea gulls come flapping in to sit on the cannery roofs to await the day of refuse. They sit on the roof peaks shoulder to shoulder. From the rocks near the Hopkins Marine Station comes the barking of sea lions like the baying of hounds. The air is cool and fresh. In the back gardens the gophers push up the morning mounds of fresh damp earth and they creep out and drag flowers into their holes. Very few people are about, just enough to make it seem more deserted than it is. One of Dora's girls comes home from a call on a patron too wealthy or too sick to visit the Bear Flag. Her makeup is a little sticky and her feet are tired. Lee Chong brings the garbage cans out and stands them on the curb. The old Chinaman comes out of the sea and flap-flaps across the street and up past the Palace. The cannery watchmen look out and blink at the morning light. The bouncer at the Bear Flag steps out on the porch in his shirtsleeves and stretches and yawns and scratches his stomach. The snores of Mr. Malloy's tenants in the pipes have a deep tunnelly quality. It is the hour of the pearl—the interval between day and night when time stops and examines itself.

On such a morning and in such a light two soldiers and two girls strolled easily along the street. They had come out of La Ida and they were very tired and very happy. The girls were hefty, big breasted and strong and their blonde hair was in slight disarray. They wore printed rayon party dresses, wrinkled now and clinging to their convexities. And each girl wore a soldier's cap, one far back on her head and the other with the visor down almost on her nose. They were full-lipped, broad-nosed, hippy girls and they were very tired.

The soldier's tunics were unbuttoned and their belts were threaded through their epaulets. The ties were pulled down a little so the shirt collars could be unbuttoned. And the soldiers wore the girls' hats, one a tiny yellow straw boater with a bunch of daisies on the crown, the other a white knitted half-hat to which medallions of blue cellophane adhered. They walked holding hands, swinging their hands rhythmically. The soldier on the outside had a large brown paper bag filled with cold canned beer. They strolled softly in the pearly light. They had had a hell of a time and they felt good. They smiled delicately like weary children remembering a party. They looked at one another and smiled and they swung their hands. Past the Bear Flag they went and said "Hiya," to the bouncer who was scratching his stomach. They listened to the snores from the pipes and laughed a little. At Lee Chong's they stopped and looked into the messy display window where tools and clothes and food crowded for attention. Swinging their hands and scuffing their feet, they came to the end of Cannery Row and turned up to the railroad track. The girls climbed up on the rails and walked along on them and the soldiers put their arms around the plump waists to keep them from falling. Then they went past the boat works and turned down into the park-like property of the Hopkins Marine Station. There is a tiny curved beach in front of the station, a miniature beach between little reefs. The gentle morning waves licked up the beach and whispered softly. The fine smell of seaweed came from the exposed rocks. As the four came to the beach a sliver of the sun broke over Tom Work's land across the head of the bay and it gilded the water and made the rocks yellow. The girls sat formally down in the sand and straightened their skirts over their knees. One of the soldiers punched holes in four cans of beer and handed them around. And then the men lay down and put their heads in the girls' laps and looked up into their faces. And they smiled at each other, a tired and peaceful and wonderful secret.

From up near the station came the barking of a dog —the watchman, a dark and surly man, had seen them and his black and surly cocker spaniel had seen them. He shouted at them and when they did not move he came down on the beach and his dog barked monotonously. "Don't you know you can't lay around here? You got to get off. This is private property!" .

The soldiers did not even seem to hear him. They smiled on and the girls were stroking their hair over the temples. At last in slow motion one of the soldiers turned his head so that his cheek was cradled between the girl's legs. He smiled benevolently at the caretaker. "Why don't you take a flying fuggut the moon?" he said kindly and he turned back to look at the girl.

The sun lighted her blonde hair and she scratched him over one ear. They didn't even see the caretaker go back to his house.

BIG SUR

Henry Miller

"A potpourri did I say? Why yes." That's how Henry Miller describes his *Big Sur and the Oranges of Hieronymous Bosch*. Published in 1957, it's a book about Henry Miller's years on the spectacular Big Sur coast of Monterey—"on the slopes of the Santa Lucia, where to give thanks to the Creator comes natural and easy." *Big Sur* tells of many things: Miller himself, his neighbors, his friends and his enemies, his visitors (both welcome and unwelcome), the artists (both real and would-be), the loafers, the dreamers, the bums; plus the sun, the sea, the fogs, the highway, and the hills. Miller's children, his wives (at least two of them), his publishers, and his critics also enter, and there's even a bit about Hieronymous Bosch and fixing the cesspool at Miller's hillside cabin. This brilliant hodgepodge—from which the following excerpts are taken—should be read by anyone who's ever been to Big Sur, or who ever intends to be there, if only in the imagination. The book was started as a pamphlet—but it grew, to the great good fortune of the reader.

Now and then a visitor will remark that there is a resemblance between this coast, the South Coast, and certain sections of the Mediterranean littoral; others liken it to the coast of Scotland. But comparisons are vain. Big Sur has a climate of its own and a character all its own. It is a region where extremes meet, a region where one is always conscious of weather, of space, of grandeur, and of eloquent silence.

From our perch, which is about a thousand feet above the sea, one can look up and down the coast a distance of twenty miles in either direction. The highway zigzags like the Grande Corniche. Unlike the Riviera, however, here there are but few houses to be seen. The old-timers, those with huge landholdings, are not eager to see the country opened up. They are all for preserving its virginal aspect. How long will it hold out against the invader? That is the big question.

The stretch of scenic highway referred to earlier was cut through at enormous expense, literally blasted out of the mountain side. It now forms part of the great international highway which will one day extend from the northern part of Alaska to Tierra del Fuego. By the time it is finished the automobile, like the mastodon, may be extinct. But the Big Sur will be here forever, and perhaps in the year A.D. 2,000 the population may still number only a few hundred souls. Perhaps, like Andorra and Monaco, it will become a Republic all its own. Perhaps the dread invaders will not come from other parts of this continent but from across the ocean, as the American aborigines are said to have come. And if they do, it will not be in boats or in airplanes.

And who can say when this region will once again be covered by the waters of the deep? Geologically speaking, it is not so long ago that it rose from the sea. Its mountain slopes are almost as treacherous as the icy sea in which, by the way, one scarcely ever sees a sail boat or a hardy swimmer, though one does oc-

casionally spot a seal, an otter or a sperm whale. The
sea, which looks so near and so tempting, is often difficult to reach. We know that the Conquistadores were
unable to make their way along the coast, neither could
they cut through the brush which covers the mountain slopes. An inviting land, but hard to conquer. It
seeks to remain unspoiled, uninhabited by man.

Often, when following the trail which meanders over
the hills, I pull myself up in an effort to encompass
the glory and the grandeur which envelops the whole
horizon. Often, when the clouds pile up in the north
and the sea is churned with white caps, I say to myself: "This is the California that men dreamed of years
ago, this is the Pacific that Balboa looked out on from
the Peak of Darien, this is the face of the earth as the
Creator intended it to look."

But *now*, now when I watch the youngsters playing
in our front yard, when I see them silhouetted against
the blue white-capped Pacific, when I stare at the huge,
frightening buzzards swirling lazily above, circling, dip-
ping, forever circling, when I observe the willow gent-
ly swaying, its long fragile branches drooping ever
lower, ever greener and tenderer, when I hear the frog
croaking in the pool or a bird calling from the bush,
when I suddenly turn and espy a lemon ripening on a
dwarfish tree or notice that the camellia has just begun
to bloom, I see my children set against an eternal
background. They are not even *my* children any
longer, but just children, children of the earth . . . and
I know they will never forget, never forsake, the place
where they were born and raised. In my mind I am
with them as they return from some distant shore to
gaze upon the old homestead. My eyes are moist with
tears as I watch them moving tenderly and reverently

amid a swarm of golden memories. Will they notice, I
wonder, the tree they were going to help me plant
but were too busy then having fun? Will they stand
in the little wing we built for them and wonder how
on earth they ever fitted into such a cubicle? Will they
pause outside the tiny workroom where I passed my
days and tap again at the windowpane to ask if I will
join them at play—*or must I work some more?* Will
they find the marbles I gathered from the garden and
hid so that they would not swallow them? Will they
stand in reverie at the forest glade, where the little
stream prattles on, and search for the pots and pans
with which we made our make-believe breakfast before
diving into the woods? Will they take the goat path
along the flank of the mountain and look up in wonder
and awe at the old Trotter house teetering in the wind?
Will they run down to the Rosses, if only in memory,
to see if Harrydick can mend the broken sword or
Shanagolden lend us a pot of jam?

For every wonderful event in my golden childhood
they must possess a dozen incomparably more wonderful. For not only did they have their little playmates,
their games, their mysterious adventures, as did I,
they had also skies of pure azure and walls of fog
moving in and out of the canyons with invisible feet,
hills in winter of emerald green and in summer mountain upon mountain of pure gold. They had even more,
for there was ever the unfathomable silence of the forest, the blazing immensity of the Pacific, days drenched
with sun and nights spangled with stars and—"Oh,
Daddy, come quick, see the moon, it's lying in the
pool!" And besides the adoration of the neighbors, a
dolt of a father who preferred wasting his time playing
with them to cultivating his mind or making himself
a good neighbor. Lucky the father who is merely a
writer, who can drop his work and return to child-

hood at will! Lucky the father who is pestered from
morn till sundown by two healthy, insatiable youngsters! Lucky the father who learns to see again through
the eyes of his children, even though he become the
biggest fool that ever was!

——— ▸◂ ◆ ◂◂ ———

It was "one of those days" when a woman with
whom I had exchanged some correspondence arrived
from Holland. My wife had only recently left me and
I was alone with my little girl. She was only in the
room a few minutes when I sensed that an instantaneous and mutual antipathy had sprung up between the
two. I apologized to my visitor for continuing with the
chores—I had decided to wash the floor and wax it—
and felt most grateful when she offered to do the dishes
for me. Meanwhile Val, my daughter, was making
things even more difficult than usual; she seemed to
take a perverse delight in interrupting our conversation,
erratic as it was with all the hopping about I was doing. Then she went to the toilet, only to announce a
moment later that it wouldn't flush. At once I dropped
the mop, dashed for the pickaxe, and began removing
the dirt which covers the septic tank. I had hardly
begun when it started to rain. I continued nevertheless,
somewhat annoyed, I confess, by my visitor's frequent
comings and goings, by her hysterical exhortations to
abandon the task. Finally I managed to get my arm
into the inlet which, as usual, was encrusted with
snarled roots. As I pulled the blockage away, out
came the water—and with it what had been dropped in
the toilet bowl. I was a pretty sight when I came back to
the house to clean up. The floor, of course, was a mess,
and the furniture still piled on the table and the bed.
My visitor, who had built up a picture of me as a
world-famous writer, a man living apart in that sublime

place called Big Sur, began to berate me—or perhaps she thought she was consoling me—for trying to do so many things which had nothing to do with my work. Her talk sounded so absurd to me that, somewhat flabbergasted, I asked her curtly who she thought was to do the dirty work . . . *God?* She continued in her vague way to dwell on what I ought not to be doing, meaning cleaning, cooking, gardening, taking care of a child, fixing cesspools and so on. I was getting hot under the collar when suddenly I thought I heard a car pull up in the turn around. I stepped outside and, sure enough, there was Varda tripping down the steps, followed by his usual retinue of friends and admirers.

"Well, well! How are you? What a surprise!"

Handshakes, introductions all around. The usual exclamations. "What a marvelous place!" (Even in the rain.)

My visitor from Holland drew me aside. With an imploring look she whispered: "What do we do now?"

"Put a good face on it," I said, and turned my back on her.

A few minutes later she tugged at my sleeve again to inquire plaintively if *I* would have to prepare a meal for all these people.

I skip what followed during the next few hours to give you her parting words: "I never dreamed that Big Sur was like this!"

Under my breath I added: "Nor did I!"

———— ◦◦ ◦◦◦ ◦◦ ————

When first I beheld this wondrous region I thought to myself—"Here I will find peace. Here I shall find the strength to do the work I was made to do."

Back of the ridge which overshadows us is a wilderness in which scarcely anyone ever sets foot. It is a great forest and game reserve intended to be set apart forever. At night one feels the silence all about, a silence which begins far back of the ridge and which creeps in with the fog and the stars, with the warm valley winds, and which carries in its folds a mystery as deep as the earth's own. A magnetic, healing ambiance. The advent of city folk, with their cares and worries, is pure dissonance. Like the lepers of old, they come with their sores. Whoever settles here hopes that he will be the last invader. The very look of the land makes one long to keep it intact—the spiritual reserve of a few bright spirits.

Of late I have come to take a different view of it. Walking the hills at dawn, or at dusk, looking over the deep canyons or seaward toward the far horizon, absorbed in reveries, drowned in the awesome beauty of it all, I sometimes think how wonderful will be the day when all these mountain sides are filled with habitations, when the slopes are terraced with fields, when flowers burst forth everywhere, not only wild flowers but flowers planted by human hands for human delectation. I try to imagine what it may be like a hundred, five hundred, years hence. I picture villas dotting the slopes, and colossal stairways curving down to the sea where boats lie at anchor, their colorful sails unfurled and flapping listlessly in the breeze. I see ledges cut into the sharp flanks of the cliffs, to give purchase to chapels and monasteries suspended between heaven and earth, as in Greece. I see tables spread under brilliant awnings (as in the time of the Doges), and wine flowing into golden goblets, and over the glitter of gold and purple I hear laughter, laughter like pearling rapids, rising from thousands of jubilant throats. . . .

Yes, I can visualize multitudes living where now there are only a few scattered families. There is room here for thousands upon thousands to come. There would be no need for a Jake to deliver food and mail three times a week. There would be ways and means undreamed of today. It could happen, in fact, in a very few years from now. What we dream *is* the reality of tomorrow.

This place can be a paradise. It is now, for those who live it. But *then* it will be another paradise, one in which all share, all participate. The *only* paradise, after all.

Peace and solitude! I have had a taste of it, even here in America. Ah, those first days on Partington Ridge! On rising I would go to the cabin door and, casting my eyes over the velvety, rolling hills, such a feeling of contentment, such a feeling of gratitude was mine that instinctively my hand went up in benediction. Blessings! Blessings on you, one and all! I blessed the trees, the birds, the dogs, the cats, I blessed the flowers, the pomegranates, the thorny cactus, I blessed men and women everywhere, no matter on which side of the fence they happened to be.

That is how I like to begin each day. A day well begun, I say. And that is why I choose to remain here, on the slopes of the Santa Lucia, where to give thanks to the Creator comes natural and easy. Out yonder they may curse, revile and torture one another, defile all the human instincts, make a shambles of creation (if it were in their power), but here, no, here it is unthinkable, here there is abiding peace, the peace of God, and the serene security created by a handful of good neighbors living at one with the creature world, with noble, ancient trees, scrub and sagebrush, wild lilac and lovely lupin, with poppies and buzzards, eagles and humming birds, gophers and rattlesnakes, and sea and sky unending.

Big Sur, California
May, 1955–June, 1956

ABOUT THE EDITORS

Although Davis and Judith Dutton currently live in Colorado, they have spent most of their lives in California and have been visiting and reading about the Monterey Peninsula for many years. Davis is currently executive editor of *Colorado Magazine*. He was previously editor of *Westways Magazine* in Los Angeles and has edited two other books for Comstock editions—*San Diego and the Back Country* and *Missions of California*. The Duttons have two small children and make their home in Denver.

A TOUCH OF
OREGON

Ralph Friedman

This is the latest verse in a continuing love song to the state and history of Oregon. It sends you on a pilgrimage along rugged coasts, across desert and wheatfields, through orchards and up majestic mountains.

But more than that, it explores the dimensions of the people—men and women of a unique breed, whose characters have been given special expression by life in a magnificent state—whose destinies have been touched by Oregon.

$1.75

A COMSTOCK EDITION

To order by mail, send price of book plus 25¢ per order for handling to Ballantine Cash Sales, P.O. Box 505, Westminster, Maryland 21157. Please allow three weeks for delivery.